Nearing The End of The Beginning
Matthew 24:8

Are these the last days?

A look at God's Prophetic Calendar

Ray James

Nearing The End of the Beginning
Ray James

Published By Parables
October, 2019

All Rights Reserved. No part of this book may be reproduced or utilized in any form or by any means, electronic or mechanical, including photocopying, recording, or by any information storage and retrieval system, without permission in writing from the author.

ISBN 978-1-951497-04-0
Printed in the United States of America

Readers should be aware that Internet Web sites offered as citations and/or sources for further information may have been changed or disappeared between the time this was written and the time it is read.

Nearing The End of the Beginning
Matthew 24:8

Are these the last days?

A look at God's Prophetic Calendar

Ray James

About the Author

Reverend Ray James is an ordained minister and has pastored in Illinois, Pennsylvania, Maryland, and Virginia. He has a Bachelor's Degree in Theology, a Master's Degree in Pastoral Ministry, and a Doctorate in Ministry. Dr. James is a pastor, author, teacher, conference speaker, and international preacher who has traveled to over 40 countries on five continents, and across 49 states in the United States. While serving in the United States Air Force on a Special Operations, Black Ops assignment, he had the unique opportunity to watch Biblical prophecy being fulfilled; which gave him the desire to write this book. He, and his wife, Linda, reside in North Carolina. They have two adult children, eight grandchildren, and four great-grandchildren.

TABLE OF CONTENTS
"NEARING THE END OF THE BEGINNING"

Table of Contents

Chapter	Title	Page
1.	Prologue	3
2.	First Things First	7
3.	The Rapture	11
4.	Our New Glorified Body	17
5.	The Judgment Seat of Christ	25
6.	The Marriage and Marriage Supper	35
7.	The Great Tribulation	45
8.	The Second Coming	71
9.	The Millennial Reign	85
10.	Satan's Last Stand	103
11.	The Great White Throne Judgment	109
12.	The Eternal State	121
13.	The Final Recorded Words of Christ	133
14.	Book Review. The Short Version	135

Chapter 1

Prologue

One day as Jesus was walking out of the temple in Jerusalem; his disciples came to him to express their appreciation for the beauty of the buildings. Without a doubt Jesus startled them by replying that one day those buildings would be torn down, and not one stone would be left in place.

Apparently there was further discussion regarding His comments as they walked out of Jerusalem on the eastern side, across the Kidron Valley and up to the Mount of Olives. In their gospels, Matthew, Mark, and Luke don't go into the detail of their conversation on the way to the Mount of Olives, but it is obvious that Jesus must have told them that the destruction of the temple would coincide with an end-time cataclysmic event in which Jesus would come back to them.

As was their custom, when they arrived at the Mount of Olives they gathered around their teacher, sat down, and leaned in to hear more of this fascinating story. Finally, they could wait no longer, they must know, and privately began to ask Him, "When is this going to happen? How will we know? Will there be some signs that we should look for?"

They must have been overwhelmed as Jesus began to catalog all of the events that would precede this event: imposters claiming to be Him, wars, threats of other wars, nations and kingdoms going to war against each other, famines with multitudes starving to death, all sorts of diseases, and the ground shaking and tremoring.

Although they had already seen much of this, His emphasis must have been on unprecedented proportions to what they had witnessed.

What captures my attention is what Matthew says (Matthew 24:8), and Mark echoes (Mark 13:8): "All these are the beginning of sorrows."

Permit me to unpack two of those words, "beginning" and "sorrows".

First, "beginning": There have been hundreds of wars since WWII. As I am writing this, there are at least 40 wars ongoing, in which over 1,000 people die each year (those in which fewer die are not included). There have been very few days of peace since this occasion of Jesus speaking to His disciples.

Famines? Over the course of the 20th century famine was virtually eradicated from most of the world. Nevertheless, during this same period some of the worst famines ever have been recorded, due to poverty, drought, totalitarian regimes, and war.

Earthquakes have now become a daily occurrence. At the time of this writing, there were 174 earthquakes worldwide in the past 24 hours, and 63,385 earthquakes in the past year (measuring 1.5 or greater on the Richter scale).

According to falseprophetsteachers.blogspot.com, thousands of people have claimed to be Jesus Christ, in our generation alone.

Let's move on to the second word, "sorrows":

The Greek word used here (Odin) is used to describe the travail or birth pains of a woman during childbirth. These "labor pains" (sorrows) will usher in the new era. The Apostle Paul uses the same metaphor in Romans 8:22 to set the stage for the new dispensation to come.

In other words, all of the events outlined in Matthew 24:5-7 are only a prelude of the things to come.

Permit me to paraphrase here, Jesus said, "This is just the beginning of the birth pains to usher in the 'new creation' of the ages and dispensations to come."

In the following chapters let's take a chronological review of where we have been, and look at where we are going.

RAY JAMES

Chapter 2

First Things First

We've all heard the expression, "Let's keep the main thing, the main thing," right? Well that's my objective, to progress from the conversation Jesus had with His disciples that beautiful sunny day on the Mount of Olives, as He began to prepare them for the things to come.

However, before we can progress into the future, I believe it's important for us to take a glance at the past to see what has brought us to this time and place.

In a chronological timeline of creation, I'm sure we would all agree that Genesis 1:1 comes first. "In the beginning God created the heaven and the earth."

Isaiah 45:18 says, "For thus saith the Lord that created the heavens; God himself that formed the earth and made it; he hath established it, he created it not in vain, he formed it to be inhabited: I am the Lord; and there is none else." Notice, He formed it to be inhabited.

And, inhabited it was; by the dinosaurs and Neanderthal man, and such. Carbon dating and other scientific methods confirm they existed. The Jurassic Period was the second segment of the Mesozoic Era. It is believed to have occurred from 199.6 to 145.5

million years ago, following the Triassic Period and preceding the Cretaceous Period. But then, something happened.

Genesis 1:2 tells us "And the earth was without form, and void; and darkness was upon the face of the deep...". Ask yourself, why would God create something without form, and void? He wouldn't.

Let's look further. Isaiah 24:1 says, "Behold, the Lord maketh the earth empty, and maketh it waste, and turneth it upside down, and scattereth abroad the inhabitants thereof." If you do a word study on the word "maketh", you will find it means to "recreate."

Let's go still further. Jeremiah 4:23-27 says, "I beheld the earth, and, lo, it was without form, and void; and the heavens, and they had no light. I beheld the mountains, and, lo, they trembled, and all the hills moved lightly. I beheld, and, lo, there was no man, and all the birds of the heavens were fled. I beheld, and, lo, the fruitful place was a wilderness, and all the cities thereof were broken down at the presence of the Lord, and by his fierce anger. For thus hath the Lord said, The whole land shall be desolate; yet will I not make a full end."

This would be the ideal place to insert the fall of Satan (Luke 10:18). Can you imagine his frustration and turmoil, as he sat upon a chaotic earth for a ga-zillion years while God contemplated restoring the heavens and earth, for His good pleasure.

Accordingly, next we pick up the story with Genesis 1:3 – 2:3. When God turned the light back on, and recreated all things. Isaiah 45:18 says, "For thus saith the Lord that created the heavens; God himself that formed the earth and made it; he hath established it, he created it not in vain, he formed it to be inhabited: I am the Lord; and there is none else."

Theologians and historians who are much smarter than I am, have concluded by tracing the genealogies of the Bible, and other validated transcripts, that the date of the recreation was Sunday, March 27, 3976 BC. (I throw that in for those who like specific timelines.) That was 5995 years ago (as of this writing).

From that date, we have the following Dispensations:

The Dispensation of Innocence. From Genesis 2:7 – 3:21, which lasted a couple of weeks, in the Garden of Eden.

The Dispensation of Conscience. Which began with man having the knowledge of good and evil. Lasting 1656 years from Adam's fall to the time of Noah's flood.

The Dispensation of Human Government. For the next 427 years from the Flood to Abraham's call. This period included earth's reinhabitation/repopulation, the Tower of Babel and the origin of languages.

The Dispensation of Promise. For 430 years, from Abraham's call to the Exodus from Egypt.

The Dispensation of Law. For 1718 years from the Exodus, and the Ten Commandments, and the rise and fall of the Roman Empire, to the birth of Jesus our Messiah.

This brings us to our current Dispensation of Grace, also known as The Church Age. From the birth of Jesus, the Christ, this will last until seven years after the Rapture of the Church.

Following our current Dispensation of Grace will be the Dispensation of Divine Government, which will last for 1,000 years of the Millennial Reign of Jesus Christ here on earth.

Finally, The Perfect Age, for the Christian, eternity forever, with our Lord and Savior.

But first, the Rapture! In the next chapter, we'll take a detailed look at what will be involved with this event.

Ray James

Chapter 3

The Rapture

The word "Rapture" is never used in the Bible. Nevertheless, by definition, it is the calling away of the saints of God to heaven.

Let's divide this chapter into four segments:

1. What is the Rapture?
2. Who will be involved in the Rapture?
3. When will the Rapture take place?
4. What will be the results of the Rapture?

1. What is the Rapture?

Literally, it means to be transported from one place to another.

1 Corinthians 15:51 – 53 says, "Behold, I shew you a mystery; We shall not all sleep, but we shall all be changed, In a moment, in the twinkling of an eye, at the last trump: for the trumpet shall sound, and the dead shall be raised incorruptible, and we shall be changed. For this corruptible must put on incorruption, and this mortal must put on immortality."

The Apostle Paul is telling the Christians that we will not "sleep", referring to those who are dead and in the grave, but "we" (those who have accepted Christ as their Savior) will be changed. Then he describes the change as having corruptible put on incorruption and mortal putting on immortality; and he says it will happen "in the twinkling of an eye". Don't confuse the "twinkling" with a "blink". I'm told the "twinkling" is one-fiftieth of one second.

Those who have accepted Jesus as their Savior will be raptured in one-fiftieth of a second. There won't be any time to ask forgiveness and repent of sins.

1 Thessalonians 4:14-18 says, "For if we believe that Jesus died and rose again, even so them also which sleep in Jesus will God bring with him. For this we say unto you by the word of the Lord, that we which are alive and remain unto the coming of the Lord shall not prevent them which are asleep. For the Lord himself shall descend from heaven with a shout, with the voice of the archangel, and with the trump of God: and the dead in Christ shall rise first: Then we which are alive and remain shall be caught up together with them in the clouds, to meet the Lord in the air: and so shall we ever be with the Lord. Wherefore comfort one another with these words."

Those saints of God whose bodies are in the grave will be raptured first, then the living will be raptured, and we will all together meet our Lord and Savior in the sky; and be with Him forever.

Then Paul ends by telling us his words should bring us comfort.

2. Who will be involved?

    A. Jesus Christ Himself, the One Who gave Himself as the propitiation of our sins. (The groom will meet His bride in the air.)

B. The Archangel, according to 1 Thessalonians 4:16. As a side note Jewish mythology states that Gabriel is always God's messenger. Nevertheless, I (personally) believe Michael will be the archangel here, because he is very much involved in "end time" prophesy. Daniel 12:1 says, "And at that time shall Michael stand up, the great prince which standeth for the children of thy people: and there shall be a time of trouble, such as never was since there was a nation even to that same time: and at that time thy people shall be delivered, every one that shall be found written in the book." (The "time of trouble" will be the Great Tribulation, and, "the book" is the Lamb's Book of Life.)

C. Every Christian who has already died. 1 Thessalonians 4:16 mentions the "dead", and, 1 Corinthians 15:52 also mentions the "dead". That would include the murdered victim, buried in a shallow grave; the aborted baby thrown into a dumpster; the cremated woman whose ashes were spread in her garden; and the sailor who was buried at sea. God will find them all, and call them home. What an exciting time it will be!

D. Every Christian who is still living (1 Thess. 4:17). I believe with my friend, Reverend Don Brankel, we are living in the terminal generation. Earth's gravity is about ready to release us.

E. Every child who has not reached the age of accountability. That would include babies in their mother's womb, and those who are mentally impaired or challenged, or too young and incapable of making an intelligent decision.

3. When will the Rapture take place?

When it comes to the debate of pre-tribulation, mid-tribulation, or post-tribulation, permit me to share my rationale for believing in a pre-trib rapture.

Daniel 12:1 says, "And at that time shall Michael stand up, the great prince which standeth for the children of thy people: and there shall be a time of trouble, such as never was since there was a nation even to that same time: and at that time thy people shall be delivered, every one that shall be found written in the book."

The Great Tribulation will be a period of God pouring out His wrath upon the world, which I believe fulfills the statement "and there shall be a time of trouble, such as never was since there was a nation even to that same time".

Wrath is defined as fury, madness, annoyance and anger.

I believe the Word of God shows us we will be spared from this wrath in Romans 5:9, 1 Thessalonians 1:10, 1 Thessalonians 5:9, and others.

The Bible is full of typologies, symbolisms and metaphors. Is the story of Lot and his family found in Genesis 19, where the angel removes him from the city to outside the city, a typology of the rapture? Was God preparing to pour out His wrath on Sodom and Gomorrah? Did He save Lot (supernaturally) from that wrath? (Genesis 19:15 & 16) I believe so.

Did God save Noah and his family from the wrath that destroyed the earth, before it started to rain? Not after it got knee high (mid-trib?)

Also, of significant importance is the fact that the church is never mentioned in the Bible during the time of the Great Tribulation on the earth. The church is mentioned several times in Revelation up through chapter 5 (Rev. 2:7, 11, 17… 3:6, 13 & 22), but after that (beginning with chapter 6) when the seals are opened, and the Great Tribulation begins, the church is never again mentioned.

From chapter 6 through chapter 19, at the opening of the seals, blowing of the trumpets, and pouring of the vials, there is no mention of the church, merely a warning, "If any man have an ear, let him hear." (Rev. 13:9)

4. What will be the results of the Rapture?

   A. All Christians will be gone.

   B. All babies, small children, mentally/challenged… gone.

   C. There will be a time of havoc (wrath) on earth as never seen before.

      1. Auto/train/plane crashes
      2. Babies disappearing from nurseries and day care centers
      3. Babies leaving their mothers' wombs
      4. Ball player hits a ball to right field, and there's no one there to catch it
      5. Dinner's cooking, mom's raptured, no one home, house burns down

That's the results for then.

The results now should be comfort for the Christian. 1 Thess. 4:18 says, "Wherefore comfort one another with these words."

Knowing the Rapture can take place any day, any minute, any second, should make us want to live holy, righteous lives before God.

The real comfort to me is thinking about what will transpire in route, between our earthly dwelling place, and our heavenly home, as God clothes us in a new body, which we will have throughout all eternity.

We'll consider our new glorified body in the next chapter; it's going to be incredible!

Chapter 4

Our New Glorified Body

What will our new glorified body be like?

1. It will be like the body of Christ
2. It will be a body of flesh and bones
3. It will be recognizable
4. It will be a body in which the Spirit dominates
5. It will be unrestricted by time, space, and gravity
6. It will be an eternal body
7. It will be a glorious body

First, consider with me that we, human beings, were created as a tripartite, comprised of a body, soul and spirit. With our body we have world-consciousness; with our soul we have self-consciousness; and, with our spirit we have God-consciousness.

At the time of our salvation our soul (mind, will, emotions, & intellect) is changed. We no longer want to live to please our self, but our desire is to please God.

Further, at the time of our salvation our spirit is also changed. Ezekiel 11:19 and Ezekiel 36:26 both tell us, in part, that God "… will put a new spirit within you…". Our God-consciousness, God-awareness, is deeper and stronger, as the Holy Spirit focuses our spirit more and more on God.

However, at the time of our salvation, our body stays the same. If you had a scar on your elbow before salvation, you will still have a scar after your salvation. If you had aches and pains before salvation, barring a simultaneous healing, you will still have aches and pains after your salvation.

Salvation did not, and does not change our bodies.

But, praise God, after the Rapture of the Church, even our bodies will be changed!

First Corinthians 15:51 – 53 says, "Behold, I shew you a mystery; We shall not all sleep, but we shall be changed, In a moment, in the twinkling of an eye, at the last trump: for the trumpet shall sound, and the dead shall be raised incorruptible, and we shall be changed. For this corruptible must put on incorruption, and this mortal must put on immortality."

The Bible does not give us a complete detailed description of our new body, but it does give us some information.

What does the Bible say about it?

1. Our new glorified body will be like the body of Christ.

This is foundational to the understanding of the other six areas mentioned previously.

Philippians 3:20 & 21 (CEV) says, "But we are citizens of heaven and are eagerly waiting for our Savior to come from there. Our Lord Jesus Christ has power over everything, and he will make these poor bodies of ours like his own glorious body."

And, John 3:2 says, "Beloved, now are we the sons of God, and it doth not yet appear what we shall be: but we know that, when he shall appear, we shall be like him; for we shall see him as he is."

Our new glorified body will be like Christ's body, as it was after His resurrection. (As a side note here, please notice the scripture says "…we shall be like him…" [meaning Christ] not like the Father, or the Holy Spirit.)

2.   Our new glorified body will be a body of flesh and bones.

In Luke 24:39, to the eleven disciples, after Jesus had risen from the grave, He said, "Behold my hands and my feet, that it is I myself: handle me, and see; for a spirit hath not flesh and bones, as ye see me have." His resurrected body had substance.

Even Job understood this, some fifteen hundred years earlier. Job 19:25 & 26 says, "For I know that my redeemer liveth, and that he shall stand at the latter day upon the earth: And though after my skin worms destroy this body, yet in my flesh shall I see God:"

That's the King James, here's the Ray James: "Though my body be vacated, one day I will stand before Him in my flesh."

3.   Our new glorified body will be recognizable.

I would submit to you that flesh and bones are recognizable, but spirits are not. Yes, spirits are discernable, but not physically recognizable.

First Corinthians 13:12 says, "For now we see through a glass, darkly; but then face to face: now I know in part; but then shall I know even as also I am known."

To me, that infers our new glorified bodies will maintain our personally distinct characteristics. In other words, we will not all be "clones" of Jesus Christ; because, if so, we would lose our personal recognition.

Now, before you disagree, let's consider another scripture. First Corinthians 15:35 – 44 says, "But some man will say, How are the dead raised up? And with what body do they come? Thou fool, that which thou sowest is not quickened, except it die: And that which thou sowest, thou sowest not that body that shall be, but bare grain, it may chance of wheat, or of some other grain: But God giveth it a body as it hath pleased him, and to every seed his own body. All flesh is not the same flesh: but there is one kind of flesh of men, another flesh of beasts, another of fishes, and another of birds. There are also celestial bodies, and bodies terrestrial: but the glory of the celestial is one, and the glory of the terrestrial is another. There is one glory of the sun, and another glory of the moon, and another glory of the stars: for one star differeth from another star in glory. So also is the resurrection of the dead. It is sown in corruption; it is raised in incorruption: It is sown a natural body; it is raised a spiritual body. There is a natural body, and there is a spiritual body."

Notice the key word repeated: "body". A body has substance, and it is recognizable. Look at that again, "…for each star differs from another… so also is the resurrection of the dead…". We will differ from one another, just as we do now. That is why we are recognizable, because we differ. Mothers of "identical" twins tell me that is true of their babies.

I guess my point here is the Bible does not say we will have some spiritual aura of discernment, in order to be able to recognize one another, so I'll leave it there.

Although we will have a glorified mind also, which will (probably) help us to recognize Moses, Abraham, Paul, Peter, John, and others.

People much smarter than I am tell me that we don't use anywhere near one-tenth of our brain today, is the other 90% being held in reserve for another day? We'll see.

4.   Our new glorified body will be a body in which the spirit dominates.

Again, 1 Corinthians 15:44 says, "It is sown a natural body; it is raised a spiritual body. There is a natural body, and there is a spiritual body."

The natural (physical) body dominates today for two reasons:

#1. We live in a three-dimensional world, in which we are conscious through our five senses of smell, taste, touch, hearing and seeing. (That is our world-consciousness.)

#2. Because of sin, it is only through our natural (carnal) body and soul that Satan can tempt us. The spirit cannot be tempted.

James 1:13-14 infers this, "Let no man say when he is tempted, I am tempted of God: for God cannot be tempted with evil, neither tempteth he any man: But every man is tempted, when he is drawn away of his own lust, and enticed."

Further, I believe Mark 14:38 confirms that our natural (physical) body can yield to temptation, but our spirit cannot, "Watch ye and pray, lest ye enter into temptation. The spirit truly is ready, but the flesh is weak."

The bottom line here is that our new glorified body will be "spirit dominated" (God-conscious); and, the flesh will always submit to the spirit in heaven.

I would also note here that God designed the spirit in man to be dominant, but sin (in the Garden of Eden) destroyed that; however, our new glorified body will correct that.

5.   Our new glorified body will be unrestricted by time, space, energy or gravity.

Remember, our new glorified body will be like Christ's resurrected body.

Jesus was able to appear and vanish before people, at will. There are stories of this in Luke's gospel, chapter 24 (look at verse 31), and John's gospel, chapter 20 (look at verses 19 and 26).

Being a spirit-controlled body, the body will be able to travel by the will of the spirit. Today our body transports our spirit; our new glorified body will be transported by our spirit.

Today, in this three dimensional world, we are limited in our transportation by time, space, energy and so forth. One day, in our new glorified bodies, there will be no restrictions.

6. Our new glorified body will be an eternal body.

Second Corinthians 5:1 says, "For we know that if our earthly house of this tabernacle were dissolved, we have a building of God, an house not made with hands, eternal in the heavens." Eternal. This new glorified body will never (ever, ever) wear out.

Always youthful (not young, just as God created Adam and Eve); always able, without limitations or disabilities

Let me say it this way: We will be in an age when age will not make a difference.

My personal belief is that a three month old aborted fetus will be matured, youthful, energetic, and full of life; and, great-grandmother's tired, wrinkled, weary body of 96 years, will be mature, yet youthful, energetic, and full of life... FOREVER!

7. Our new glorified body will be a glorious body.

Our glorified body will be glorious! Magnificent, in every way!

The Apostle Paul writes (1 Cor. 15:43), "It is sown in dishonor; it is raised in glory: it is sown in weakness; it is raised in power:"

To the Romans he wrote (Rom. 8:18), "For I reckon that the sufferings of this present time are not worthy to be compared with the glory which shall be revealed in us."

The glory of God, His glory, will be revealed in us, in our new glorified body. Permit me to illustrate that another way. The word "glorified" or "glorious" in the Greek, literally means "putting off light" or "shining".

On the Mount of Transfiguration, remember how God shown? Remember how Moses shown? On the road to Damascus, when God pulled back the curtain of heaven a little bit, and revealed Himself to Saul, how he was blinded… by the light… by His glory.

Daniel 12:2-3 says, "And many of them that sleep in the dust of the earth shall awake, some to everlasting life, and some to shame and everlasting contempt. And they that turn many to righteousness as the stars for ever and ever."

Verse two uses the word, "everlasting", and verse three says "for ever and ever"; we will reflect the light of God. Just as the moon reflects the light of the Sun, we will reflect the light of the Son, forever.

No pain, no suffering. No glasses, no hearing aids. No pills, no false teeth. No surgeries, no pacemakers. I will never again hear the clicking of the prosthetic heart valve I now have in my chest. The aging process that began in the Garden of Eden will be eliminated! Terminated forever!

So far, we have looked at the Rapture of the Church, and during that transformational journey through the sky we have put on our New Glorified Body. Now, upon our arrival in heaven the Lamb's book of Life will be opened. We'll study that in the next chapter, are you ready?

RAY JAMES

Chapter 5

The Judgment Seat of Christ

As we have done in previous chapters, let's break this topic up into bite-sized pieces:

1. What is the Judgment Seat of Christ?
2. Who will be involved with the Judgment?
3. What will the Judge be concerned with?
4. What will be the results of the Judgment?

This event will immediately follow the Rapture of the Church.

I believe we will have a brief time of reunion with those who have gone on before us, prior to the Rapture; nevertheless, at this point in time of our eternal future, time will not stand still, and there will be much to be accomplished during this seven year period, while the Great Tribulation is taking place on the earth.

1. What is the Judgment Seat of Christ?

This is the judgment where all believers will stand before Jesus and will give an account for their stewardship (of time, talents, treasure, et cetera).

In Romans 14:10-12 the Apostle Paul is writing to the saints in Rome (1:7), and says, "But why dost thou judge thy brother? Or why dost thou set at nought thy brother? For we shall all stand before the judgment seat of Christ. For it is written, As I live, saith the Lord, every knee shall bow to me, and every tongue shall confess to God. So then every one of us shall give account of himself to God."

Again, writing to the saints in Corinth (2 Co. 1:1) the Apostle Paul writes in 2 Corinthians 5:10, "For we must all appear before the judgment seat of Christ; that every one may receive the things done in his body, according to that he hath done, whether it be good or bad." (Notice Paul is including himself, when he says "we" must all appear before the judgment seat of Christ.)

To help give this a better perspective, let's remember to whom Paul is writing, and the culture of that day. The phrase "Judgment Seat" actually comes from the Greek word "Bema", which was commonly used during that time. I have had the privilege of visiting a couple of ancient Olympic arenas in Greece and Israel, and have stood on the raised platform in those arenas where the athletes and Olympians stood to receive their rewards, after being judged for their performance.

After the game or sporting event, the athletes would walk over to, and stand in front of, the Bema platform; this is where the winners would receive their rewards.

Remember the culture to which Paul is writing. In 63 BC Caesarea was freed by Pompey, and given to Herod the Great, who spent twelve years building a city and coliseum for Caesar Augustus, for Olympic Games and sporting activities. The court of Areopagus at Mars Hill in Greece is another great example of this.

Only winners stood before the Bema Seat, and, accordingly, only Christians will stand before the Bema Seat, which is the Judgment Seat of Christ, to receive their reward(s).

2.   Who will be involved in the Judgment Seat of Christ?

First, as we have already seen, will be the raptured believers from time and eternity past, dead and remaining. Every believer will appear at this Judgment Seat.

Secondly, the Judge, who according to John 5:22 will be Jesus Christ, Himself. "For the Father judgeth no man, but hath committed all judgment unto the Son:".

The most knowledgeable, respected, righteous, judge there could ever be. The One, Who according to Hebrews 4:15 knows what we have been through, "For we have not an high priest which cannot be touched with the feeling of our infirmities; but was in all points tempted like as we are, yet without sin."

3. What will our Judge, Jesus Christ, be concerned with at this Judgement?

First, note, he will not be concerned with punishing the believer for sin. The believer's sins have already been dealt with, through our confession and repentance, because of the redemptive work through the shed blood of Jesus on the cross of Calvary, which, according to Hebrews 8:12 and 10:17, He will remember no more.

However, He will be concerned with how we, as Christians, conducted ourselves concerning our stewardship while here on earth.

First Peter 4:10 says, "As every man hath received the gift, even so minister the same one to another, as good stewards of the manifold grace of God." Notice the word "the" gift. God gives us "the" gift that pleases Him, which He desires for us, specifically, and personally, to have; versus "a" gift, which is non-specific.

Also, 1 Corinthians 4:1 & 2 says, "Let a man so account of us, as of the ministers of Christ, and stewards of the mysteries of God. Moreover it is required in stewards, that a man be found faithful." Our stewardship is not optional, it is required, and we will be held accountable for it at the Judgment Seat of Christ.

A steward, as Peter and Paul are describing here, is a person who was given charge over a large household, or an estate. He was to keep things going in a manner which would please the owner, or lord, of the property. In other words, in a manner in which the owner himself would have done things.

We will be judged according to how we have managed ourselves according to our privileges and responsibilities as His stewards, whether we have been faithful (managed well), or, been unfaithful (mismanaged).

What have we done with the gifts, talents, and abilities that God has given to us? What have we done with His Son? (The Parable of the Talents in Matthew 25 and Luke 19 is an excellent illustration of this.)

What are some of the specifics that Christ will be concerned with?

Why did we do the things we did? What was our reason? What was our motive?

Many good works will go up in smoke, because they were done for ungodly or selfish reasons. First Corinthians 3:13 says, "Every man's work shall be made manifest: for the day shall declare it, because it shall be revealed by fire; and the fire shall try every man's work of what sort it is."

First Corinthians 4:5 also says, "Therefore judge nothing before the time, until the Lord come, who both will bring to light the hidden things of darkness, and will make manifest the counsels of the hearts: and then shall every man have praise of God." The word "counsels" used here means "thought, intent, or purpose". Christ will make manifest what was in our hearts, when we did what we did.

The question we need to constantly remind ourselves of is, are we working for God, or, are we working for man's attention?

Conversely, not only is Jesus going to be concerned with the reasons for which we have done some things, but He will also be concerned with why we didn't do other things. Remember, a faithful steward gets the job done. Not just part of it, but all of it, just as if he was the lord of it.

James 4:17 says, "Therefore to him that knoweth to do good, and doeth it not, to him it is sin." You may ask God's forgiveness for this, and go to heaven, but you will still give an account for why you didn't do what you should have done.

Jesus will also be concerned with what we did with the right motives, which, I would submit to you is the primary purpose of this judgement. Rewards!

Remember, in a pre-tribulation rapture, the Judgment Seat of Christ will continue for up to seven years. This is a serious Judgment, and our Judge, Jesus Christ won't miss anything.

Let me insert a gentle reminder here: We must accomplish what God wants us to do, as good stewards, with the right motives; and not worry about what others think, and be more concerned with pleasing Jesus, the Lord of all.

4. What are the results of the Judgment Seat of Christ?

    A. Some will suffer loss. They will lose their reward, because of motive, or disobedience.

First Corinthians 3:15 says, "If any man's work shall be burned, he shall suffer loss: but he himself shall be saved; yet so as by fire." The Amplified Bible says it this way, "But if any person's work is burned up [by the test], he will suffer the loss [of his reward]; yet he himself will be saved, but only as [one who has barely escaped] through fire."

Every good work done for the wrong reason will have no reward; the reward was given on earth, through the accolades of man.

      B. Some will not receive every reward Jesus had stored for them.

Second John 8 says, "Look to yourselves, that we lose not those things which we have wrought, but that we receive a full reward."

Without a doubt God has purposed for us His blessings and benefits as His children, just as we have purposed good gifts to our children. Nevertheless, the actions of our children sometimes restrict us from giving them the blessings we desired to give to them. The same is true with our Heavenly Father.

God has given us many opportunities to receive His rewards, which we have rejected for a myriad of reasons (stated previously), and will not be rewarded for them.

Let me illustrate it this way: If we have a 40 hour work week, and receive ten dollars an hour, at the end of the week (pre-tax) we would have $400. However, if we decide to go in late one hour every day that week, for 35 hours we would only be paid $350. By our own choice we lost the reward of $50. The same is true of our spiritual "timeclocks".

      C. We will receive reward for what we have done.

First Corinthians 3:14 says, "If any man's work abide which he hath built thereupon, he shall receive a reward."

We did what we were asked to do, and our motives were right. The reward will be given.

We keep using the word reward, or rewards; but, what are they. I'm not sure I could speak to all of the rewards, but I do see five specific rewards that are mentioned in the Bible, so let's look at them.

1. The Incorruptible Crown

First Corinthians 9:25 – 27 says, "And every man that striveth for the mastery is temperate in all things. Now they do it to obtain a corruptible crown; but we an incorruptible. I therefore so run, not as uncertainly; so fight I, not as one that beateth the air: But I keep under my body, and bring it into subjection: lest that by any means, when I have preached to others, I myself should be a castaway."

It appears the Incorruptible Crown will be rewarded to those who overcome the selfish and sinful desires of the old nature, and keep their flesh under subjection.

2. The Crown of Rejoicing

First Thessalonians 2:18 – 20 says, "Wherefore we would have come unto you, even I Paul, once and again, but Satan hindered us. For what is our hope, or joy, or crown of rejoicing? Are not even ye in the presence of our Lord Jesus Christ at his coming? For ye are our glory and joy."

It appears the Crown of Rejoicing is given to the soul-winners, who have won others to the Lord; rejoicing over those who have been saved. If the Great Commission is to "Go Make Disciples", and the first step of discipleship is evangelism, I would suggest to you, that God has intended for every Christian to be rewarded with this crown. The question is: Will you be?

3.   The Crown of Life

Revelation 2:10 says, "Fear none of those things which thou shalt suffer: behold, the devil shall cast some of you into prison, that ye may be tried; and ye shall have tribulation ten days; be thou faithful unto death, and I will give thee a crown of life."

Apparently, the Crown of Life will be given to those who have overcome times of trial and intense suffering which has cost them their life. Beginning with the first century disciples of Jesus, right down to the present day, we are very much aware of an untold number of men and women that have given their lives for the cause of Christ; some privately, and some publically.

We weep now, when we hear of those who have, and will, give their life for their faith; and, I believe we will weep again at the Judgment Seat of Christ, as the Crown of Life is rewarded to these saints of God.

4.   The Crown of Righteousness

Second Timothy 4:6 – 8 the Apostle Paul writes, "For I am now ready to be offered, and the time of my departure is at hand. I have fought a good fight, I have finished my course, I have kept the faith: Henceforth there is laid up for me a crown of righteousness, which the Lord, the righteous judge, shall give me at that day: and not to me only, but unto all them also that love his appearing." Notice that phrase, "to all them also that love his appearing". The NIV says, "to all who have longed for his appearing".

I have observed, and possibly you have too, some nominal Christians who are simply carrying on with life, enjoying each day, and are not particularly "longing" for the appearance of Jesus at the Rapture of the Church. Then, again, there are those who are daily crying out "even so come quickly Lord Jesus", and who are truly, in the strictest sense of the word, "longing for His appearance".

To those who are watching the eastern sky, looking and longing, a Crown of Righteousness will be given.

5.   The Crown of Glory

First Peter 5:2 – 4 says, "Feed the flock of God which is among you, taking the oversight thereof, not by constraint, but willingly; not for filthy lucre, but of a ready mind; Neither as being lords over God's heritage, but being examples to the flock. And when the chief Shepherd shall appear, ye shall receive a crown of glory that fadeth not away."

Apparently reserved for those preachers and teachers and disciplers, who have been diligent to feed their flocks; faithful to study and teach the uncompromising Word of God; to them, will be given the Crown of Glory.

Now, fasten your spiritual seatbelts here, and give me permission to provoke your thought. Will these five crowns be literal crowns, as we see worn on the heads of royalty? Will they be the ones cast at the feet of Jesus? If so, it will be a "one-time event" that will soon be over.

According to Encarta Dictionary, in addition to being an ornate headdress worn as a symbol of sovereignty, success, or high achievement, a "crown" is also a title or distinction that signifies victory of supreme achievement.

Could these five crowns simply be a special title, honor, or position that could be used throughout eternity to glorify God? I'm of the opinion they could be. Revelation 4:10 & 11 says, "The four and twenty elders fall down before him that sat on the throne, and worship him that liveth for ever and ever, and cast their crowns before the throne, saying, Thou art worthy, O Lord, to receive glory and honour and power: for thou hast created all things, and for thy pleasure they are and were created."

Remember, in our Glorified Body, we are no longer living a life that is all about us, but, rather, our spirit has now resumed the dominant position that God has always intended, and there are no longer the selfish "me" attitudes. We will fully desire to glorify, praise, honor, and worship the Lord, and what better way than joining the four and twenty elders in returning any crowns we may receive by title or distinction, to the One deserving all glory and honor, by casting our "crowns" at His feet also.

>   D. Finally, what are the Results of the Judgment Seat of Christ (that could, or should, be present in our lives today)?

Knowing that every one of us will one day give an account of our lives (obedience, disobedience, commission, omission, motives, thoughts, idle words, etc.) before Jesus Christ, should make us want to live every day pleasing to God!

First John 2:28 says, "And now, little children, abide in him; that, when he shall appear, we may have confidence, and not be ashamed before him at his coming."

One of the reasons the Corinthian Church kept having trouble was because they kept forgetting that one day they were going to stand in judgment. I pray we, the modern-day church, will not make the same mistake.

Seven literal years for the Rapture of the Church, for us to be clothed in the uniqueness of our Glorified Body, and stand before Jesus at the Judgment Seat of Christ, is a very long time. What else will transpire with the Church in heaven, during the Great Tribulation here on earth? It will be a time of celebration like we have never seen before.

Come on, turn the page, you know you want to.

Chapter 6

The Marriage, and The Supper of the Lamb

Let's segment this one also.

1. The Proof of the Marriage
2. The Place of the Marriage
3. The Participants of the Marriage
4. The Pattern of the Marriage

Weddings always seem to bring excitement to the participants. There are lots of plans and preparations, sometimes taking a year, or longer. We want everything to be perfect.

The exciting point to this marriage, is that it has taken all of eternity past, to prepare.

What we are going to be looking at in this chapter is the "Wedding of all Weddings". It should also bring excitement to us.

There will be no expense spared, because the father of the bride has unlimited resources.

There will be no prenuptial agreements needed, because this marriage will last for all eternity.

There will be no cold feet because this will be the most desired marriage of all the ages.

1. The Proof of the Marriage

The best way to prove anything is through the Word of God – It is the Truth.

Romans 7:4 says, "Wherefore, my brethren, ye also are become dead to the law by the body of Christ; that ye should be married to another, even to him who is raised from the dead, that we should bring forth fruit unto God."

Paul, speaking to the church, says, as the body of Christ (the Church/Bride), you are no longer yoked to the law (and to the world), but you are soon to be married to another, to the One Who was raised from the dead.

In 2 Corinthians 11:2 we see two stages of the planned marriage, spoken by the Apostle Paul to the church (the Bride), regarding the engagement/betrothal and the presentation of the bride, "For I am jealous over you with godly jealousy: for I have espoused you to one husband, that I may present you as a chaste virgin to Christ."

Further proof of the marriage is found in Revelation 19:7-9, "Let us be glad and rejoice, and give honour to him: for the marriage of the Lamb is come, and his wife hath made herself ready. And to her was granted that she should be arrayed in fine linen, clean and white: for the fine linen is the righteousness of saints. And he saith unto me, Write, Blessed are they which are called unto the marriage supper of the Lamb. And he saith unto me, These are the true sayings of God."

Prophesying far into the future, the Prophet Isaiah wrote (61:10), "I will greatly rejoice in the Lord, my soul shall be joyful in my God; for he hath clothed me with the garments of salvation, he hath covered me with the robe of righteousness, as a bridegroom decketh himself with ornaments, and as a bride adorneth herself with her jewels."

Obviously, there are many scriptures in both the Old and New Testaments which attest to the coming Marriage and Marriage Supper of the Lamb.

2. The Place of the Marriage

Let's first consider this as to the place in time, following the Judgment Seat of Christ, and before the Second Coming of Christ, after all of the matters of the judgment and rewards are behind us.

Then, let's consider the geographical place. Obviously, we are still in heaven at this time, and the marriage will take place there, because it is from heaven that we will return to this earth after the marriage according to Revelation 19:11 "And I saw heaven opened, and behold a white horse; and he that sat upon him was called Faithful and True, and in righteousness he doth judge and make war." Then, verse 14, "And the armies which were in heaven followed him upon white horses, clothed in fine linen, white and clean".

"…Clothed in fine linen, white and clean". That's how the bride was described in verse 8. The church/the bride will be descending from heaven. So, the wedding of all weddings, will take place in the place of all places, heaven. Not after we return to earth, as some have suggested.

Remember, this is still during the period of the Great Tribulation, here on earth.

3. Who are the Participants in this Marriage?

A. God the Father will certainly be there. He is the host. He's the One Who has already sent out the invitations: Luke 14:16-23, "Then said he unto him, A certain man made a great supper, and bade many: And sent his servant at supper time to say to them that were bidden, Come; for all things are now ready. And they all with one consent began to make excuse. The first said unto him, I have bought a piece of ground, and I must needs go and see it: I pray thee have me excused. And another said, I have married a wife, and therefore I cannot come. So that servant came, and shewed his lord these things. Then the master of the house being angry said to his servant, Go out quickly into the streets and lanes of the city, and bring in hither the poor, and the maimed, and the halt, and the blind. And the servant said, Lord, it is done as thou hast commanded, and yet there is room. And the lord said unto the servant, Go out into the highways and hedges, and compel them to come in, that my house may be filled."

There appears to be plenty of room around the supper table, that God the Father has already invited us to.

B. If you're going to have a marriage, you have to have a bridegroom.

And, that is our Lord and Savior, Jesus the Christ!

John the Baptist pointed that out in John 3:27 – 30, "John answered and said, A man can receive nothing, except it be given him from heaven. Ye yourselves bear me witness, that I said, I am not the Christ, but that I am sent before him. He that hath the bride is the bridegroom: but the friend of the bridegroom, which standeth and heareth him, rejoiceth greatly because of the bridegroom's voice: this my joy therefore is fulfilled. He must increase, but I must decrease."

John identifies Jesus as the bridegroom, and then Jesus identifies Himself as the bridegroom, in Luke 5:32-35, "I came not to call the righteous, but sinners to repentance. And they said unto him, Why do the disciples of John fast often, and make prayers, and likewise the disciples of the Pharisees; but thine eat and drink?

And he said unto them, Can ye make the children of the bridechamber fast, while the bridegroom is with them? But the days will come, when the bridegroom shall be taken away from them, and then shall they fast in those days."

    C. If you're going to have a marriage, you have to have a bride.

Ephesians 5:22 – 32 says, "Wives, submit yourselves unto your own husbands, as unto the Lord. For the husband is the head of the wife, even as Christ is the head of the church: and he is the saviour of the body. Therefore as the church is subject unto Christ, so let the wives be to their own husbands in every thing. Husbands, love your wives, even as Christ also loved the church, and gave himself for it; That he might sanctify and cleanse it with the washing of water by the word, That he might present it to himself a glorious church, not having spot or wrinkle, or any such thing; but that it should be holy and without blemish. So ought men to love their wives as their own bodies. He that loveth his wife loveth himself. For no man ever yet hated his own flesh; but nourisheth and cherisheth it, even as the Lord the church: For we are members of his body, of his flesh, and of his bones. For this cause shall a man leave his father and mother, and shall be joined unto his wife, and they two shall be one flesh. This is a great mystery: but I speak concerning Christ and the church."

Every believer from the Day of Pentecost, will be a part of the precious bride of Jesus Christ.

    D. Then we have a fourth group of people, and we'll call them the invited guests.

You've got to have witnesses and spectators, to help you celebrate this special occasion. But who are these witnesses and spectators?

Revelation 19:9 tells us, "And he saith unto me, Write, Blessed are they which are called unto the marriage supper of the Lamb. And he saith unto me, These are the true sayings of God."

The bride has already been identified in verses seven and eight, so, who are "the called" of verse nine?

Let's look again at John 3:29, "He that hath the bride is the bridegroom: but the friend of the bridegroom, which standeth and heareth him, rejoiceth greatly because of the bridegroom's voice: this my joy therefore is fulfilled."

Who is this friend, or these friends, the called? Many believe it will be the early saints before the Spirit's calling beginning at the Day of Pentecost; and, others believe it will be the angels in heaven.

Consider this: As great as Noah, Abraham, Isaac, Jacob, David, Daniel, Deborah, Ruth, and all of the sainted dead, both Jews and Gentiles (mainly Jews)... as great as these men and women were, yet they are not a part of the New Testament Church. (The key words here are "New Testament".)

There are only three references to the church in the Gospel according to Matthew, and all other references are found in the Epistles and Revelation. Clearly, "the Church" began after the Day of Pentecost.

Before we leave this topic, give thought to the eleventh chapter of the Epistle of Hebrews with me. After cataloging many of the exploits of the Old Testament saints in the first thirty-eight verses of this chapter, the writer go on to make a very bold statement in verses 39 and 40. I quote from The Message, "Not one of these people, even though their lives of faith were exemplary, got their hands on what was promised. God had a better plan for us: that their faith and our faith would come together to make one completed whole, their lives of faith not complete apart from ours."

With consideration to this, I believe the "friends", the invited guests, the "called" will be the Old Testament saints.

E. The Pattern of the Marriage

We appear to already be following the pattern of a traditional New Testament wedding. The three stages are:

1. The Betrothal Stage. (Selection and promise of marriage)
2. The Presentation Stage.
3. The Celebration Stage.

1. The Betrothal

Before the foundations of the world, God decided His Son should have a bride; and the church is His betrothed. The declaration was made.

According to Ephesians 1:3 & 4, we have been chosen: "Blessed be the God and Father of our Lord Jesus Christ, who hath blessed us with all spiritual blessings in heavenly places in Christ: According as he hath chosen us in him before the foundation of the world, that we should be holy and without blame before him in love:"

Then, 1 Corinthians 6:19 & 20 explain the dowry, or payment made: "What? Know ye not that your body is the temple of the Holy Ghost which is in you, which ye have of God, and ye are not your own? For ye are bought with a price: therefore glorify God in your body, and in your spirit, which are God's."

Peter describes that "price" in 1 Peter 1:18 & 19: "Forasmuch as ye know that ye were not redeemed with corruptible things, as silver and gold, from your vain conversation received by tradition from your fathers; But with the precious blood of Christ, as of a lamb without blemish and without spot:".

2. The Presentation

In the traditional New Testament custom the father would send for the bride and the bride would be brought to the house. (Picture the Rapture here in your mind.)

Then, at the right time the father would present the bride to his son by placing their hands together.

The presentation stage will take place at the Rapture of the Church, when we are called to the Father's house to meet His Son face to face... and, at the right time our hand will be placed in His.

Consider it like this: The Father will call us to His house and "present you" (Jude 24 & 2 Corinthians 11:2) "to Christ". (In 2 Co. 11:2 we see both the betrothal and the presentation.)

3. The Celebration

The celebration of a public marriage supper was the occasion of John 2, where Jesus turned the water into wine, in Cana. The supper was actually the celebration that followed the actual marriage, or exchanging of vows.

After the marriage in heaven has been performed, we will go to the celebration table, where Christ Himself (the Bridegroom) will prepare Himself, make Himself ready, gird His loins; and Christ Himself will serve us, just as the groom serves his bride.

Luke describes this in another story (12:37): "Blessed are those servants, whom the lord when he cometh shall find watching: verily I say unto you, that he shall gird himself, and make them to sit down to meat, and will come forth and serve them."

Can you imagine how unworthy that will make us feel, as Christ, the Great Servant, begins to serve us, His bride?

Just for "grins and giggles" before we shift gears and go to the next topic, do you have any idea what will be on the menu at this supper? Revelation 2:7 says, "He that hath an ear, let him hear what the Spirit saith unto the churches; To him that overcometh will I give to eat of the tree of life, which is in the midst of the paradise of God." What do you think?

Now remember, during the past seven years we have been caught up in the Rapture, put on our new Glorified Body, stood before Jesus at the Judgment Seat of Christ, and celebrated our marriage at the Marriage Supper of the Lamb; and during this time on earth, those who were left have been going through a terrible time of wrath that the Bible calls The Great Tribulation.

Get ready, and hang on tight, because the Bible has much to say about what will be happening here on earth, while we have been in heaven.

Ray James

Chapter 7

The Great Tribulation

As has been our practice so far, let's break this chapter down into bite-sized subtopics to make it easier to digest.

1. The Titles of the Tribulation
2. The Purpose of the Tribulation
3. The Mark of the Tribulation
4. The 144,000 of the Tribulation
5. The 2 Witnesses of the Tribulation
6. The Action of the Tribulation

Before we delve into this topic, let me mention this is not intended, nor will it be, a complete study of everything the Bible has to say about The Great Tribulation.

Now, remember, we have already concluded that immediately following the Rapture of the Church, the Great Tribulation period will begin here on earth.

Also remember, the period of the Great Tribulation on earth is still during the Age or Dispensation of Grace.

Thus the title of this book, "Nearing the End of the Beginning". The Great Tribulation will be the end of the beginning of sorrows spoken of in Matthew 24:8 and Mark 13:8;

and what a time of sorrows it will be. I am so glad a way of escape has been made for the church, and we are not going to be here.

1. The Titles of the Tribulation

   A. The Tribulation (Matthew 24:21 & 29)
   B. A Time of Trouble (Daniel 12:1)
   C. The Overspreading of Abominations (Daniel 9:27)
   D. The Indignation (Isaiah 26:20 & 34:2)
   E. The Hour of His Judgement (Rev. 14:6 & 7)
   F. The Great Day of His Wrath (Rev. 6:17)
   G. The Time of the End (Daniel 12:9)
   H. The Seventieth Week (Daniel 9:24-27)
   I. The Great Day of the Lord (Zeph. 1:14 & Joel 2:11)
   J. The Time of Jacob's Trouble (Jeremiah 30:7)
   K. The Day of God's Vengeance (Isaiah 34:8 & 63:4)

The point here is to understand the Great Tribulation is referred to by many titles and the events of those titles. Knowing these titles will help you in your own study, so as to not confuse these titles with other, separate, events. They are all the same event, the period of the Great Tribulation.

For the purpose of this book, however, we are going to use the title by which it is most commonly called and known by: The Great Tribulation.

2. The Purpose of the Great Tribulation

Without a doubt, God has a plan and a purpose for everything He does or permits to happen.

   A. The primary purpose of the Great Tribulation is to prepare Israel, the Jews, for their Messiah. Certainly, it has always been His plan and His purpose to bring His people to their Messiah.

Let's briefly consider a scripture, and, I'll make an observation, and then I'll leave this for you to study further, on your own should you desire.

Zechariah 13:8-9 says, "And it shall come to pass, that in all the land, saith the Lord, two parts therein shall be cut off and die; but the third shall be left therein. And I will bring the third part through the fire, and will refine them as silver is refined, and will try them as gold is tried: they shall call on my name, and I will hear them: I will say, It is my people: and they shall say, The Lord is my God."

It is only natural for me to believe the 1st part is when Rome invaded Israel and killed at least two-thirds of the Jews. The 2nd part will probably be the rejection of Judaism (which must occur); which will leave the 3rd part: Christianity, (vs 9) refined and left to rule with Jesus as we enter into the Millennial Reign.

If you disagree, that's fine. To be honest and transparent, sometimes I even disagree with myself; but when trying to determine the plan and purpose of God for His people, this just makes sense to me.

Again, the primary purpose for the Great Tribulation is to prepare Israel (the Jews) to meet their Messiah; and, obviously, Judaism must be rejected for that to happen. I realize Judaism will not be totally abolished, because not all Jews will accept Christ as their Messiah, any more than all Gentiles will accept Jesus as their redeemer and savior.

Another purpose for the Great Tribulation is:

B. To pour out His judgments on the unrighteous.

Romans 1:18 says, "For the wrath of God is revealed from heaven against all ungodliness and unrighteousness of men, who hold the truth in unrighteousness;".

Second Thessalonians 2:9 – 12 says, "Even him, whose coming is after the working of Satan with all power and signs and lying wonders, And with all deceivableness of unrighteousness in them that perish; because they received not the love of the truth, that they might be saved. And for this cause God shall send them strong delusion, that they should believe a lie: That they all might be damned who believed not the truth, but had pleasure in unrighteousness."

The delusion spoken of here will (among other lies) be a lie that will be told as the reason for the disappearance of millions of people (Christians), and God's wrath will be punishment for believing this lie.

The first half of the week (Daniel's 70th week) will be a time when Satan, through the Antichrist, will have full authority to rule the world. Then, after the lies have been believed by people, the Antichrist will expose himself for who he really is, and God will pour out His wrath upon the world to punish the nations (Matthew 25) for their iniquity. But never forget, it will be done in such a way as to draw Israel (the Jews) back to Christ.

We don't have all the details of how that will be accomplished, but we do understand the Bible to tell us it will be absolutely devastating. It will be an awesome display of the power of God.

3. The Mark of the Tribulation

I certainly don't want to downplay the significance of the Mark of the Tribulation, however, I believe most people seem to be overly concerned with this part, more than anything else; and, I would submit to you this part is really least significant, in my opinion. Permit me to explain.

For those who remember, when O.J. Simpson was on trial for murder, the defending battery of attorneys put Mark Furman in the spotlight for many months. The more Furman was in the spotlight, the less Simpson was. The trial turned from: who killed Nicole Simpson and Ron Goldman, to: Mark Furman is a racist. The jury, and America, lost sight of the true issue!

The same thing happened with Bill Clinton. By their defense, the attorneys attempted, by accusations, to put Ken Starr, Monica Lewinsky and Linda Tripp on trial, to take the attention off Bill Clinton.

I believe the more our enemy can get our attention on something as insignificant as the Mark, the less we will be concerned with being ready for the Rapture (which is the real issue).

The Mark of course is: 666. Revelation 13:16 – 18 says, "And he causeth all, both small and great, rich and poor, free and bond, to receive a mark in their right hand, or in their foreheads: And that no man might buy or sell, save he that had the mark, or the name of the beast, or the number of his name. Here is wisdom. Let him that hath understanding count the number of the beast: for it is the number of a man; and his number is Six hundred threescore and six."

I am intrigued by the statement in verse 18 that says, "count the number". Not "read" the number, but count it. Counting shows a progression, doesn't it?

Typically, on a barcode, which is a code consisting of a series of vertical bars of variable width and height that are scanned by a laser, printed on a product (insert "person") to identify the item (again, insert person), the character/symbol used at the beginning, middle, and end of the number is the character of the number six (two thin vertical lines).

The accountability and capability of the barcode is virtually unlimited in its application and already being used internationally, even in third-world countries; and, it is easy to conceive that a barcode, or something similar, will be incorporated into the Mark.

Personally, it doesn't matter to me what the Mark will be; I simply would refuse to have anything stamped on my hand or forehead, and implanted under the skin, which is now being done with "chips".

What we do know about the Mark (Rev. 13:17) is that you cannot buy or sell anything without having the Mark. No food, gas, heating oil, diapers, nothing! And once a person receives the Mark, their eternal fate will be sealed.

Okay, we know:

A. The number is a number of a man, it is an incomplete number (6).

B. It will be required if you want to buy/sale/trade anything during the Great Tribulation.

C. This Mark will invoke God's wrath.

Revelation 16:1 & 2 says, "And I heard a great voice out of the temple saying to the seven angels, Go your ways, and pour out the vials of the wrath of God upon the earth. And the first went, and poured out his vial upon the earth; and there fell a noisome and grievous sore upon the men which had the mark of the beast, and upon them which worshipped his image."

During the last half (three and one-half years) of the Great Tribulation, God's wrath will be poured out upon all the earth, and will affect everyone. Then, according to this scripture, there will be a part of God's wrath that will be specifically targeted to those with the Mark.

D. The Mark will seal a person's fate.

Revelation 14:9-11 says, "And the third angel followed them, saying with a loud voice, If any man worship the beast and his image, and receive his mark in his forehead, or in his hand, The same shall drink of the wine of the wrath of God, which is poured out without mixture into the cup of his indignation; and he shall be tormented with fire and brimstone in the presence of the holy angels, and in the presence of the Lamb: And the smoke of their torment ascendeth up for ever and ever: and they have no rest day nor night, who worship the beast and his image, and whosoever receiveth the mark of his name."

Plainly said, if a person accepts the Mark, they will have just sold their soul to Satan with an irrevocable contract.

4. The 144,000 of the Tribulation.

Revelation 7:1-4 says, "And after these things I saw four angels standing on the four corners of the earth, holding the four winds of the earth, that the wind should not blow on the earth, nor on the sea, nor on any tree. And I saw another angel ascending from the east, having the seal of the living God: and he cried with a loud voice to the four angels, to whom it was given to hurt the earth and the sea, Saying, Hurt not the earth, neither the sea, nor the trees, till we have sealed the servants of our God in their foreheads. And I heard the number of them which were sealed: and there were sealed an hundred and forty and four thousand of all the tribes of the children of Israel."

Who are they? Jews, of the 12 tribes of Israel. The specific numbers of each tribe are stated in verses 5 through 8; 12,000 of each.

As I am sure you have, I too have heard well-meaning people, of various church denominations say that the number represents the total number of people that will be going to heaven. How sad, that's simply not true.

The 144,000 are:

A. Jews, "From the tribes of Israel".

B. "Servants of God" (verse 3)

C. They are specifically selected of God for a particular purpose. Revelation 14:1-4 says, "And I looked, and, lo, a Lamb stood on the mount Sion, and with him an hundred forty and four thousand, having his Father's name written in their foreheads. And I heard a voice from heaven, as the voice of many waters, and as the voice of a great thunder: and I heard the voice of harpers harping with their harps: And they sung as it were a new song before the throne, and before the four beasts, and the elders: and no man could learn that song but the hundred and forty four thousand, which were redeemed from the earth. These are they which were not defiled with women; for they are virgins. These are they which follow the Lamb whithersoever he goeth. These were redeemed from among men, being the firstfruits unto God and to the Lamb."

The 144,000 will have a specific ministry: "And this gospel of the kingdom shall be preached in all the world for a witness unto all nations; and then shall the end come." (Matthew 24:14) "And then shall the end come", the end of this dispensation, the Age of Grace. The Church Age.

These 144,000 will preach "Endure to the end, and then Christ will return"... the 2nd Coming, to set up His Divine Government, the next dispensation, the Millennial Reign.

D. Then, also notice with me that these 144,000 have a "special place"... set apart, according to Revelation 14:3, "These are they which follow the Lamb...".

Remember, billions have not yet heard the gospel. Hindus, Buddhists, Muslims, from every nation on earth, even right here in the United States of America. I'm told that 80,000 babies were born last night, in India alone.

The 144,000 will be responsible for reaching "a great multitude, which no man could number, of all nations, and kindreds, and people, and tongues..." (Rev. 7:9)

5. The 2 Witnesses of the Tribulation.

Revelation 11:3 says, "And I will give power unto my two witnesses, and they shall prophesy a thousand two hundred and threescore days, clothed in sackcloth."

These two witnesses will appear on the scene immediately after the Rapture of the Church, and they will probably be responsible for the salvation of the 144,000, that we just looked at, who will scatter throughout the entire world.

Did you notice verse 3 said they would prophesy for 1260 days? That period is 18 days short of half the period of the Great Tribulation. We will later see where the Great Tribulation is separated in halves, and, so, may I suggest it appears as if there will be a 17 or 18 day transitional period.

Let's just go ahead now, and try to guess who these two witnesses may be. Some contend they are probably Elijah and Enoch. Why? Because Elijah and Enoch never died, and "it is appointed unto men once to die" according to Hebrews 9:27. Remember Elijah was taken up in a whirlwind, and Enoch was "translated that he might not see death".

Nevertheless, these two men have very special power. Revelation 11:5 & 6 says, "And if any man will hurt them, fire proceedeth out of their mouth, and devoureth their enemies: and if any man will hurt them, he must in this manner be killed. These have power to shut heaven, that it rain not in the days of their prophecy: and have power over waters to turn them to blood, and to smite the earth with all plagues, as often as they will."

Whoa!!! Does the comment about the rain remind you of Elijah? Does the comment about the plagues remind you of Enoch? No, but it does remind me of Moses. Why did Satan dispute with the archangel Michael (Jude 9) over the body of Moses? To keep him from a future work?

We don't know, but here's what we do know:

A. These two have a special power. (Rev. 11:5 & 6)

B. These two men will be the light of Christ on the earth. (Rev. 11:4)

C. They will have a limited time. Revelation 11:7 says, "And when they shall have finished their testimony, the beast that ascendeth out of the bottomless pit shall make war against them, and shall overcome them, and kill them." (If Elijah and Enoch, this will be their "appointed time to die".

D. They will receive no further respect. (Because of the deception of Satan.) Revelation 11:8-10 says, "And their dead bodies shall lie in the street of the great city, which spiritually is called Sodom and Egypt, where also our Lord was crucified. And they of the people and kindreds and tongues and nations shall see their dead bodies three days and an half, and shall not suffer their dead bodies to be put in graves. And they that dwell upon the earth shall rejoice over them, and make merry, and shall send gifts one to another; because these two prophets tormented them that dwelt on the earth."

ABC/NBC/CBS/CNN/FOX/CSPAN, will all have their cameras on these two men, and will be broadcasting, "These two trouble-makers are finally dead", and the sinners and scoffers will be dancing in the street. But, wait a minute…

E. They will have a big surprise. Revelation 11:11 & 12 says, "And after three days and a half the spirit of life from God entered into them, and they stood upon their feet; and great fear fell upon them which saw them. And they heard a great voice from heaven saying unto them, Come up hither. And they ascended up to heaven in a cloud; and their enemies beheld them."

Surprise!!! They will ascend up into heaven, and the 144,000 will continue the work they started, by spreading the gospel story throughout the world.

6. The Action of the Tribulation

There are a lot of things that we could look at specifically regarding the Great Tribulation, such as the person of the Antichrist, the Beast and False Prophet, and so forth. I don't want to go into too much detail, though, or this book would be over 1,000 pages.

Nevertheless, Revelation chapters 6 through 19 cover the period of the Great Tribulation, in addition to many other references throughout the Old and New Testaments, and I want to briefly consider parts of those chapters.

Although many things will happen simultaneously, I want to attempt to look at the Great Tribulation chronologically, as much as possible.

The beginning of the Great Tribulation will be a relatively peaceful time, compared to what will develop. It will begin with the Antichrist appearing on the scene to promote international, and national peace, and to balance budgets. However, any peace brought about will be short-lived.

The Prophet Daniel's description of the invasion of the Roman Empire against the Eastern Nations is actually a typology of what will follow this peaceful time.

Daniel 11:36 – 45 says, "[36] And the king shall do according to his will; and he shall exalt himself, and magnify himself above every god, and shall speak marvelous things against the God of gods, and shall prosper till the indignation be accomplished: for that that is determined shall be done. [37] Neither shall he regard the God of his fathers, nor the desire of women, nor regard any god: for he shall magnify himself above all. [38] But in his estate shall he honour the God of forces: and a god whom his fathers knew not shall he honour with gold, and silver, and with precious stones, and pleasant things. [39] Thus shall he do in the most strong holds with a strange god, whom he shall acknowledge and increase with glory: and he shall cause them to rule over many, and shall divide the land for gain. [40] And at the time of the end shall the king of the south push at him: and the king of the north shall come against him like a whirlwind, with chariots, and with horsemen, and with many ships; and he shall enter into the countries, and shall overflow and pass over. [41] He shall enter also into the glorious land, and many countries shall be overthrown: but these shall escape out of his hand, even Edom, and Moab, and the chief of the children of Ammon. [42] He shall stretch forth his hand also upon the countries: and the land of Egypt shall not escape. [43] But he shall have power over the treasures of gold and of silver, and over all the precious things of Egypt: and the Libyans and the Ethiopians shall be at his steps. [44] But tidings out of the east and out of the north shall trouble him: therefore he shall go forth with great fury to destroy, and utterly to make away many. [45] And he shall plant the tabernacles of his palace between the seas in the glorious holy mountain; yet he shall come to his end, and none shall help him."

Obviously the Antichrist will be one of the greatest men of all time. He will be an economic, political, military, and religious genius.

Second Thessalonians 2:3 & 4 says, "Let no man deceive you by any means: for that day shall not come, except there come a falling away first, and that man of sin be revealed, the son of perdition; Who opposeth and exalteth himself above all that is called God, shewing himself that he is God." And verses 9 & 10 say, "Even him, whose coming is after the working of Satan with all power and signs and lying wonders, And with all deceivableness of unrighteousness in them that perish; because they received not the love of the truth, that they might be saved."

It is safe to say, the Antichrist will be convincing.

He's going to make a peace treaty with Israel, which is supposed to last seven years, but he's going to break it, half way through. Daniel 9:27 says, "And he shall confirm the covenant with many for one week: and in the midst of the week he shall cause the sacrifice and the oblation to cease, and for the overspreading of abominations he shall make it desolate, even until the consummation, and that determined shall be poured upon the desolate." (A week, spoken of here is a period of seven years.)

The first 3 ½ years will be of peace, but will only serve to be a calm before the storm. At this point we begin in the sixth chapter of Revelation, with the opening of the Seals. (Why "seals"? Because a seal keeps something undisclosed until the appropriate time to reveal.)

Revelation 6:1 & 2 says, "And I saw when the Lamb opened one of the seals, and I heard, as it were the noise of thunder, one of the four beasts saying, Come and see. And I saw, and behold a white horse: and he that sat on him had a bow; and a crown was given unto him: and he went forth conquering, and to conquer."

The Antichrist will appear on a white horse, and he has a bow, but notice he has no arrows. In other words, he will have victory, without a battle. There will be no bloodshed at this time. He will be well-liked, with enticing words… a smooth operator.

This is when an international covenant will be made with the nations of the world. A one-world monetary system and one-world government are foreseeable here with other sweeping changes.

Then the second seal is opened. Let's read about it, Revelation 6:3 & 4, "And when he had opened the second seal, I heard the second beast say, Come and see. And there went out another horse that was red: and power was given to him that sat thereon to take peace from the earth, and that they should kill one another: and there was given unto him a great sword."

Just as the white horse represents a period of peace, as much as three and one-half years later (probably after the covenant with Israel is broken), a rider on a red horse appears carrying a sword and has the power to take away the peace from the earth. (The red horse represents blood-shed, or war.)

Soon after, the third seal is opened. Revelation 6:5 & 6 says, "And when he had opened the third seal, I heard the third beast say, Come and see. And I beheld, and lo a black horse; and he that sat on him had a pair of balances in his hand. And I heard a voice in the midst of the four beasts say, A measure of wheat for a penny, and three measures of barley for a penny; and see thou hurt not the oil and the wine."

The black horse follows the red horse. During the period of the war of the 2nd seal, the emphasis is obviously taken away from the crops and agriculture.

The black horse now represents famine.

Notice the phrase: "A measure of wheat for a penny, and three measures of barley for a penny." A penny at the time of that writing actually represented a full day's wages. In other words, a quart of wheat or three quarts of barley will cost a day's wages (IF you have taken the "Mark").

As of the date of this writing, the current Federal minimum wage is $7.25 per hour. For a typical eight hour work day, the pay before taxes would be $58. That would be today's cost for a quart of wheat or three quarts of barley, again, IF you had taken the "Mark".

But notice, the oil and the wine are not harmed. (Is the upper- or middle-class eliminated here?)

Not only will food be expensive, but remember, you will still have to have the Mark of the Beast to purchase it.

We next see the opening of the 4th Seal, in Revelation 6:7 & 8; "And when he had opened the fourth seal, I heard the voice of the fourth beast say, Come and see. And I looked, and behold a pale horse: and his name that sat on him was Death, and Hell followed him. And power was given unto them over the fourth part of the earth, to kill with sword, and with hunger, and with death, and with the beasts of the earth."

The pale horse represents death, which is the rider's name. With the advent of this fourth seal being opened one-fourth of the world's population will die of war, hunger (the famine of the 3rd seal), death (literally interpreted as "disease"), and wild animals.

Let's pause and put some of this together in a natural order of events. Will the red horse of war (2nd seal) represent a nuclear holocaust so powerful that it will destroy most of the crops around the globe (3rd seal), and chemical warfare result in the diseases of the 4th seal?

As of the time of this writing, in 2019, the world's population is estimated to be 7.7 billion. Let's imagine 1.7 billion are raptured. Six billion would enter the Great Tribulation. Twenty-five percent of six billion would be 1.5 billion souls which would die. The Bible tells us it would take seven months just to bury the dead; and I'm sure the vast majority of these would be in common graves, dug with bulldozers. (These figures are given for illustrative purposes only. Obviously no one, except God, knows the actual numbers.)

The fifth seal is next to be opened, in Revelation 6:9 – 11, which says, "And when he had opened the fifth seal, I saw under the altar the souls of them that were slain for the word of God, and for the testimony which they held: And they cried with a loud voice, saying, How long, O Lord, holy and true, dost thou not judge and avenge our blood on them that dwell on the earth? And white robes were given unto every one of them; and it was said unto them, that they should rest yet for a little season, until their fellowservants also and their brethren, that should be killed as they were, should be fulfilled."

John the Revelator is picturing here the martyrs' souls crying out, who have given their lives for the gospel. Those who have not taken the Mark of the Beast, who believed the message of the 144,000; which I would believe to conservatively be hundreds of thousands, or millions of people.

The sixth seal of Revelation 6:12 – 17 literally changes the earth's topography: "And I beheld when he had opened the sixth seal, and, lo, there was a great earthquake; and the sun became black as sackcloth of hair, and the moon became as blood; And the stars of heaven fell unto the earth, even as the fig tree casteth her untimely figs, when she is shaken of a mighty wind. And the heaven departed as a scroll when it is rolled together; and every mountain and island were moved out of their places. And the kings of the earth, and the great men, and the rich men, and the chief captains, and the mighty men, and every bondman, and every free man, hid themselves in the dens and in the rocks of the mountains; And said to the mountains and rocks, Fall on us, and hide us from the face of him that sitteth on the throne, and from the wrath of the Lamb: For the great day of his wrath is come; and who shall be able to stand?"

Now imagine this, if you can: Obviously there will be many physical changes upon the earth, and only <u>now</u> are men trying to escape the wrath of God.

Scientists and physicists tell us this is a very "literal picture" of how things would look following a nuclear world war, which we apparently saw when the 2nd seal was opened.

In order to find the seventh seal we have to skip over chapter seven, and go to Revelation chapter eight, verse one: "And when he had opened the seventh seal, there was silence in heaven about the space of half an hour."

Why do you hold your breath and refuse to speak? A few weeks ago my wife and I vacationed with our son, daughter-in-law, a few of our grandchildren, and three of our great-grandchildren. Without the details, one of the children did something very surprising, and we all held out breath. What would happen? Would the child be scolded? Would we just shrug it off and laugh so no feelings would be hurt? Why did we hold our breath? Fear. Fear of the unknown.

Revelation 8:1 says "…there was silence in heaven…". Apparently, we in heaven must be aware of what is happening, at least partially, on earth; and, apparently, we are anticipating something very catastrophic to happen.

Seven angels who have the seven trumpets are preparing themselves to sound their trumpets, then (Rev. 8:7), "The first angel sounded, and there followed hail and fire mingled with blood, and they were cast upon the earth: and the third part of trees was burnt up, and all green grass was burnt up."

Can you imagine this? Not just one-third of the trees in the woods down the street from your house, or just your neighbors grass. This is one-third of all the trees of the world, and every blade of grass around the globe.

We don't know for sure, but I would imagine this is a continuation of the perpetual war to follow, beginning with the opening of the 2nd seal.

Revelation 8:8 & 9 captures the blowing of the second trumpet: "And the second angel sounded, and as it were a great mountain burning with fire was cast into the sea: and the third part of the sea became blood; And the third part of the creatures which were in the sea, and had life, died; and the third part of the ships were destroyed."

The Greek word used here for "sea" is derived from the Greek word for "salt", and appears to be in singular form (versus plural). Does that mean a single body of water, such as the Mediterranean Sea, or all oceans (salt water)? My guess is "all" ocean water, because of what follows. Can you imagine one-third of all sea-life dying (what a stench as they float to the top); and one-third of all the ships of the world destroyed?

The third trumpet is found in Revelation 8:10 & 11, and says, "And the third angel sounded, and there fell a great star from heaven, burning as it were a lamp, and it fell upon a third part of the rivers, and upon the fountains of waters; And the name of the star is called Wormwood: and the third part of the waters became wormwood; and many men died of the waters, because they were made bitter."

This judgment now extends from the sea water (ocean, salt waters) to the fresh waters (rivers, and our drinking water); and one-third of the water turns bitter, and many die.

As if that isn't enough, just when you think it certainly couldn't get any worse, watch what follows. The fourth trumpet is contained in verses 12 and 13: "And the fourth angel sounded, and the third part of the sun was smitten, and the third part of the moon, and the third part of the stars; so as the third part of them was darkened, and the day shone not for a third part of it, and the night likewise. And I beheld, and heard an angel flying through the midst of heaven saying with a loud voice, Woe, woe, woe, to the inhabiters of the earth by reason of the other voices of the trumpet of the three angels, which are yet to sound!"

Daylight is cut off for one-third of the day, eight hours, in addition to the night, and the fourth angel is calling out, "Trouble, trouble, trouble, to everyone who lives on the earth". (CEV)

From a nuclear war, with the disease and famine that ensues, to the death of 25% of the earth's population, to one-third of the vegetation destroyed, and one-third of the salt waters and fresh water contaminated, and NOW the angel says, "Look out for what's coming"? At this point, it's hard to imagine anything worse could follow.

But with the fifth trumpet of Revelation 9:1-6, it does, "And the fifth angel sounded, and I saw a star fall from heaven unto the earth: and to him was given the key of the bottomless pit. And he opened the bottomless pit; and there arose a smoke out of the pit, as the smoke of a great furnace; and the sun and the air were darkened by reason of the smoke of the pit. And there came out of the smoke locusts upon the earth: and unto them was given power, as the scorpions of the earth have power. And it was commanded them that they should not hurt the grass of the earth, neither any green thing, neither any tree; but only those men which have not the seal of God in their foreheads. And to them it was given that they should not kill them, but that they should be tormented five months: and their torment was as the torment of a scorpion, when he striketh a man. And in those days shall men seek death, and shall not find it; and shall desire to die, and death shall flee from them."

Demon-possessed locust will torment (not kill) men that do not have the seal of God. Remember, this seal is what the 144,000 gave first, that Satan, via the Antichrist, wanted to copycat with the 666 Mark.

I cannot imagine the torment of these locusts. I have to be honest, when I am mowing my yard, and gnats are buzzing around my face, that drives me bananas… and they don't bite!

Listen to the description of these locusts (Rev. 9: 7-10) "And the shapes of the locusts were like unto horses prepared unto battle; and on their heads were as it were crowns like gold, and their faces were as the faces of men. And they had hair as the hair of women, and their teeth were as the teeth of lions. And they had breastplates, as it were breastplates of iron; and the sound of their wings was as the sound of chariots of many horses running to battle. And they had tails like unto scorpions, and there were stings in their tails: and their power was to hurt men five months."

The sixth trumpet is found in Revelation 9:13-19, "And the sixth angel sounded, and I heard a voice from the four horns of the golden altar which is before God, Saying to the sixth angel which had the trumpet, Loose the four angels which are bound in the great river Euphrates. And the four angels were loosed, which were prepared for an hour, and a day, and a month, and a year, for to slay a third part of men. And the number of the army of the horsemen were two hundred thousand thousand: and I heard the number of them. And thus I saw the horses in the vision, and them that sat on them, having breastplates of fire, and of jacinth, and brimstone: and the heads of the horses were as the heads of lions; and out of their mouths issued fire and smoke and brimstone. By these three was the third part of men killed, by the fire, and by the smoke, and by the brimstone, which issued out of their mouths. For their power is in their mouth, and in their tails: for their tails were like unto serpents, and had heads, and with them they do hurt."

Four demons are released from the Euphrates River (1,780 miles long, flowing through Turkey, Syria, Iran and Iraq [the birthplace of the Assyrian and Babylonian Empires], and emptying into the Persian Gulf), and they will lead a demonic army of two hundred million men, to kill one-third of the remaining people.

Let's see, for illustrative purposes only, we started with 7.7 billion people, and raptured 1.7 billion, leaving 6 billion people, of which 1.5 billion died following the opening of the 4th seal. That leaves 4.5 billon people, of which one-third more are killed leaving 3 billion. In less than three and one-half years, one-half of the post-rapture population will die; and that's after a period of five months, when people would seek death, and not find it. That means one-half of the world's population will die in a period of three years.

Now, let's skip over Revelation, chapter 10, and come to the blowing of the 7th trumpet in Revelation 11:15-19, "And the seventh angel sounded; and there were great voices in heaven, saying, The kingdoms of this world are become the kingdoms of our Lord, and of his Christ; and he shall reign for ever and ever. And the four and twenty elders, which sat before God on their seats, fell upon their faces, and worshipped God, Saying, We give thee thanks, O Lord God Almighty, which art, and wast, and art to come; because thou hast taken to thee thy great power, and hast reigned. And the nations were angry, and thy wrath is come, and the time of the dead, that they should be judged, and that thou shouldest give reward unto thy servants the prophets, and to the saints, and them that fear thy name, small and great; and shouldest destroy them which destroy the earth. And the temple of God was opened in heaven, and there was seen in his temple the ark of his testament: and there were lightnings, and voices, and thunderings, and an earthquake, and great hail."

The 7th trumpet brings with it the proclamation that Christ will soon return to earth, and all of heaven rejoices at this; while those on earth are angered at this news. Angered, after all they have been through… can you imagine?

The sounding of the seventh trumpet actually leads toward the pouring of the seven vials (or, bowls), found in the sixteenth chapter of Revelation. Verses 1 & 2 contain the first vial: "And I heard a great voice out of the temple saying to the seven angels, Go your ways, and pour out the vials of the wrath of God upon the earth. And the first went, and poured out his vial upon the earth; and there fell a noisome and grievous sore upon the men which had the mark of the beast, and upon them which worshipped his image."

It appears these are the same seven angels, that sounded the trumpets, and the cancerous boils are aimed at those who have taken the Mark of the Beast. There are some who believe the sores will be caused by in infection and inflammation caused by the

Mark. Although a reasonable assumption, I'm not sure I would support that theory.

What I do find interesting is the similarities to the 10 plagues of Exodus, at the pouring out of the vials.

The second vial from Revelation 16:3 says, "And the second angel poured out his vial upon the sea; and it became as the blood of a dead man: and every living soul died in the sea."

At the sounding of the second trumpet one-third of the sea (salt-water, oceans) became blood, and, now, with the pouring of the second vial, the entire oceans become blood.

At the sounding of the second trumpet one-third of the fish died, and now, the remaining fish die.

In Revelation 16:4 we find the third vial, "And the third angel poured out his vial upon the rivers and fountains of waters; and they became blood."

At the sounding of the third trumpet one-third of the fresh water became bitter; now all fresh water is contaminated.

And now, pardon the pun, the heat is on, with the pouring of the fourth vial (Rev. 16:8 & 9), "And the fourth angel poured out his vial upon the sun; and power was given unto him to scorch men with fire. And men were scorched with great heat, and blasphemed the name of God, which hath power over these plagues: and they repented not to give him glory."

Unbelievable, they blasphemed God, and "repented not".

Revelation 16:10 & 11 contains the fifth vial, "And the fifth angel poured out his vial upon the seat of the beast; and his kingdom was full of darkness; and they gnawed their tongues for pain, And blasphemed the God of heaven because of their pains and their sores, and repented not of their deeds."

The Greek word used for "seat" is "thronos" (yes, throne), implying a place of authority and power, identifying the leadership. This vial is specifically aimed at the leaders.

The sixth vial is interesting, in Revelation 16:12 – 16, "And the sixth angel poured out his vial upon the great river Euphrates; and the water thereof was dried up, that the way of the kings of the east might be prepared. And I saw three unclean spirits like frogs come out of the mouth of the dragon, and out of the mouth of the beast, and out of the mouth of the false prophet. For they are the spirits of devils, working miracles, which go forth unto the kings of the earth and of the whole world, to gather them to the battle of that great day of God Almighty. Behold, I come as a thief. Blessed is he that watcheth, and keepeth his garments, lest he walk naked, and they see his shame. And he gathered them together into a place called in the Hebrew tongue Armageddon."

During this time, the mighty lion that has divided countries since the dawn of time, from the east to the west, is dried up. The mighty Euphrates River.

This 1,780 mile river that is over one-half mile wide in places is dried up, so that the kings can cross over to get to the place called, Armageddon (in the Jezreel Valley, below Megiddo.)

These kings will be deceived by these three "frog-like" demons that will work miracles, to draw them all together, for the final massacre.

With the seventh vial, found in Revelation 16:17-21, it is finished, "And the seventh angel poured out his vial into the air; and there came a great voice out of the temple of heaven, from the throne, saying, It is done. And there were voices, and thunders, and lightnings; and there was a great earthquake, such as was not since men were upon the earth, so mighty an earthquake, and so great. And the great city was divided into three parts, and the cities of the nation fell: and great Babylon came in remembrance before God, to give unto her the cup of wine of the fierceness of his wrath. And every island fled away, and the mountains were not found. And there fell upon men a great hail out of heaven, every stone about the weight of a talent: and men blasphemed God because of the plague of the hail; for the plague thereof was exceeding great."

The great city of Babylon is torn asunder, into three pieces, islands sank into the oceans, and mountains were flattened onto the ground, and hundred pound hail stones fall from heaven. What a climactic end. But men are still blaspheming God.

Now, before moving away from the Actions of the Great Tribulation, permit me to throw a few thoughts out, for your contemplation and consideration, to wrap up this chapter.

There is a federation of nations that is forming, and has been for several years, that will actually combine and reform something like the old Roman Empire.

What we do know is: it will end up being a ten nation federation.

From the Trilateral Commission, formed by the United States, Japan, and Western Europe came the European Economic Community (EEC), also known as the Common Market (CM), later renamed the European Community (EC), and now the European Union (EU), which is comprised of the EC and two other pillars.

I'm just spit-balling these organizations because somewhere along the line, and I would predict very soon, we will see the forming of a similar government like the old Roman Empire, from which will rise a political ruler to lead this Ten Nation Federation.

This ruler is going to make a covenant with Israel, and return to them most, if not all, of their nation (Gaza Strip, Bethlehem, Hebron, West Bank, Jericho, and, yes, even part of Jerusalem.)

Take a minute to read Revelation 13:1-10.

Of course this ruler is: The Antichrist.

During the Great Tribulation there is also going to be a very powerful church on earth; no, not the church of Jesus Christ, they're gone; but, rather, a church that will worship The Beast. It will be a massive, false, religious system. You can read about this in Revelation 13:11-18.

Remember, the Antichrist will not only be a political, economic, and military genius, he will also be a religious leader.

Remember also, this is also going to be a period of great tribulation for the nation of Israel. We skipped over Revelation 11, where you can read about that.

Of course the False Church, that worships the Beast, will not last. I believe the False Church is actually symbolized by the Harlot of Revelation, chapters 17 and 18. And, in those two chapters, you can also see her ultimate destruction.

Let me also just briefly mention, we all know that Satan has access today to heaven (Job 1:6 & 7), but do you realize he will continue to have access to heaven until the middle of the Great Tribulation? He will; Revelation12:7-9 reveals that. I find that interesting, don't you?

Chapter 8

The Second Coming

Without a doubt the Rapture of the Church will be an incredibly awesome event, and I don't want to make light of it; however, I believe it will pale by comparison to the Second Coming of our Lord and Savior, Jesus Christ.

Let's consider the Second Coming in a 7 segment outline:

1. The Drum Roll
2. His Dazzling Appearance
3. Down to Earth
4. Delivering the Jews
5. Defeat at Armageddon
6. Dividing the Nations
7. Judgment of the Fallen Angels

I'm not sure words can adequately describe this event, and I'm certain I cannot adequately capture this event on these pages. Needless to say, it will be one of the greatest events on God's prophetic calendar; and, there is nothing I know of that is able to describe the glory of this day.

If you subscribe to a pre-tribulation rapture, as I do, then we know the Second Coming is at least seven years away.

At the time of the Rapture we meet Jesus in the sky. At the Second Coming He will physically return to earth to rule and reign for 1,000 years in what we know to be the Millennial Reign of Christ.

The Second Coming is actually a bridge between the Great Tribulation and the Millennial Reign.

He won't be coming to this earth the second time to be denied or crucified, He will be coming as the King of kings, and the Lord of lords; and He is coming back to establish His divine reign over all of His creation.

1. The Drum Roll

In today's society when we are awaiting the appearance of a special person or a special event, that occasion is typically preceded by a drum roll; and excitement and anticipation builds with that drum roll.

If you listen carefully, I believe you can hear that drum roll in the distance, as His Church eagerly awaits His appearance in the sky; and there will be a period of seven years when that sound will get louder and louder.

Matthew 24:29-31 says, "Immediately after the tribulation of those days shall the sun be darkened, and the moon shall not give her light, and the stars shall fall from heaven, and the powers of the heavens shall be shaken: And then shall appear the sign of the Son of man in heaven: and then shall all the tribes of the earth mourn, and they shall see the Son of man coming in the clouds of heaven with power and great glory. And he shall send his angels with a great sound of a trumpet, and they shall gather together his elect from the four winds, from one end of heaven to the other."

Notice, "...the powers of the heavens shall be shaken...". Remember as we studied the sixth and seventh judgments, represented by the sixth and seventh vials being poured out? The sixth and seventh vials are actually a part of this drum roll, where there is thunder, lightning, a mighty earthquake that causes mountains to crumble and islands to disappear, and 100-pound hail stones… immediately preceding the Second Coming.

Can you hear the drum roll? The stage will be set, for the Lord of lords to descend, for the King of kings to assume office, for the Son of God to return!

2. His Dazzling Appearance

Revelation 19:11-14 says, "And I saw heaven opened, and behold a white horse; and he that sat upon him was called Faithful and True, and in righteousness he doth judge and make war. His eyes were as a flame of fire, and on his head were many crowns; and he had a name written, that no man knew, but he himself. And he was clothed with a vesture dipped in blood: and his name is called The Word of God. And the armies which were in heaven followed him upon white horses, clothed in fine linen, white and clean."

Following the drum roll we don't see a curtain that slowly opens in the middle to reveal the person behind the scene. But, rather, following the drum roll the heavens will burst wide open, and the Son of God will descend riding a white horse. His eyes as a flame of fire, and many crowns upon His head. His robe covered with blood, either His own blood by which He has purchased our salvation, or the blood of the enemy (symbolically) He has already conquered.

Rest assured, every eye will be focused on this great event!

ABC, CBS, NBC, CNN, C-SPAN, FOX NEWS, and others, may not have been able to focus their cameras quickly enough to catch a shot of the Rapture, but I'll guarantee the entire world will be focused on this great event… The Second Coming!

This time our Lord will not be clothed with humility, but He will be clothed to go to war (against unrighteousness).

Revelation 19:14 says, in part, "The armies of heaven followed him".

The stables in heaven will release her horses, and the bride (blood-bought Christians), will follow Christ on these white horses that will gallop across the galaxies.

I believe this is what Enoch was seeing, as Jude describes in verses 14 & 15, "And Enoch also, the seventh from Adam, prophesied of these, saying, Behold, the Lord cometh with ten thousands of his saints, To execute judgment upon all, and to convince all that are ungodly among them of all their ungodly deeds which they have ungodly committed, and of all their hard speeches which ungodly sinners have spoken against him."

Those who are here during the Great Tribulation will see us returning on white horses, as the clouds roll back and heaven opens.

Revelation 1:7 says, "Behold, he cometh with clouds; and every eye shall see him, and they also which pierced him: and all kindreds of the earth shall wail because of him. Even so, Amen."

Can you hear the news casters? "Look at the sky!" To the cameraman, "Quick, get a shot of this. Somebody's coming on a white horse... no, there's more than one; there's hundreds, no thousands... no there are tens of thousands!"

This will be a dazzling appearance, of the King of kings, and Lord of lords.

Someone once asked me, "How long will it take, 10 minutes, 30 minutes, one-hour?" My reply was, I don't know, but it will be long enough for the entire world to see it!

3. Down to Earth

At this point in the chapter, Jesus Christ, and we with him, have not set foot on the earth. Where will we initially land? Where will Jesus stand? Zechariah 14:3-4 says, "Then shall the Lord go forth, and fight against those nations, as when he fought in the day of the battle. And his feet shall stand in that day upon the mount of Olives, which is before Jerusalem on the east, and the mount of Olives shall cleave in the midst thereof toward the east and toward the west, and there shall be a very great valley; and half of the mountain shall remove toward the north, and half of it toward the south."

When Jesus steps upon the Mount of Olives the earth will respond to His return with a mighty earthquake. If He hasn't already captured the world's attention, this earthquake certainly will, as Christ steps on earth again.

Now, let's go on to the fourth part, remembering, now things will happen in concert with one another, simultaneously.

4. Delivering the Jews

During the Great Tribulation the Jews will be persecuted more than any other time in history, even more than during the Holocaust when 6 million Jews were murdered. Because of this persecution many of the Jews will flee to Edom (Petra) for refuge. Although uninhabited today, the caves and cliffs in that region will make natural hiding places.

Revelation 12:6 says, "And the woman fled into the wilderness, where she hath a place prepared of God, that they should feed her there a thousand two hundred and threescore days." (Inferring here from the middle to the end of the Great Tribulation.)

When Christ returns, one of the first things He is going to do is to go to Edom, to Petra, to where the Jewish people will be. He is going to go to His friends.

He is going to appear to them as the King of kings, and the Jews will realize, He is the Messiah!

Watch this next verse, it is one of my favorite verses in all the Bible; someone will speak up and ask Jesus the question found in Zechariah 13:6, "And one shall say unto him, What are these wounds in thine hands? Then he shall answer, Those with which I was wounded in the house of my friends," and they will realize for the first time what they have done.

That's why the Bible says it will be a time of mourning, (Zechariah 12:10-11), "And I will pour upon the house of David, and upon the inhabitants of Jerusalem, the spirit of grace and of supplications: and they shall look upon me whom they have pierced, and they shall mourn for him, as one mourneth for his only son, and shall be in bitterness for him, as one that is in bitterness for his firstborn. In that day shall there be a great mourning in Jerusalem, as the mourning of Hadadrimmon in the Valley of Megiddon." But I believe it will be a bittersweet happy mourning.

At the delivering of the Jews, they will leave Edom (we call it Petra) and will be led back to Israel (and specifically Jerusalem), to turn back to the Messiah to follow and worship Him.

A few years ago a Gideon told me there is an organization of men who have already travelled to Petra and placed Bibles in the caves where they believe the Jews will flee to.

5. The Defeat at Armageddon

Revelation 19:19 says, "And I saw the beast, and the kings of the earth, and their armies, gathered together to make war against him that sat on the horse, and against his army."

Remember, Revelation 16:13-16 said, "And I saw three unclean spirits like frogs come out of the mouth of the dragon, and out of the mouth of the beast, and out of the mouth of the false prophet. For they are the spirits of devils, working miracles, which go forth unto the kings of the earth and of the whole world, to gather them to the battle of that great day of God Almighty. Behold, I come as a thief. Blessed is he that watcheth, and keepeth his garments, lest he walk naked, and they see his shame. And he gathered them together into a place called in the Hebrew tongue Armageddon."

Picture this for a minute, and follow the sequence of these events: Remember the last half of the Great Tribulation is the drum roll for the Second Coming.

Follow me here: The drying up of the Euphrates River, the earthquake and the heavens opening up and Christ appearing; all will happen relatively quickly.

Zechariah 14:1-3, says, "Behold, the day of the Lord cometh, and thy spoil shall be divided in the midst of thee. For I will gather all the nations against Jerusalem to battle; and the city shall be taken, and the houses rifled, and the women ravished; and half of the city shall go forth into captivity, and the residue of the people shall not be cut off from the city. Then shall the Lord go forth, and fight against those nations, as when he fought in the day of battle."

The largest army ever assembled, will be gathered together in a place called (Har)-Megiddo, (Armageddon), and Satan is the head of this mighty army. He will use these three "frog-like" demon creatures (Rev. 16:13 & 14), that come up out of the Euphrates River; and he uses them, through their miracles, to gather together all the armies of the world.

What are they gathering to do? To go to Edom, and kill the Jews. Remember, by now the Antichrist has convinced the entire world to hate the Jews. However, also remember, the Jews have already been delivered by Christ; but they are only just now preparing to leave Edom.

Now, let's hit the pause button for just a minute to consider what is just about to happen, as these armies are gathering together in the Jezreel Valley at Megiddo, ready to go to war against Israel. This could very well be the only war in history where there are no casualties on the winning side, and the losing army will suffer complete defeat! Not because of tanks or guns, or atomic or nuclear weapons, but by the sword that comes out of the mouth of Christ.

Revelation 1:16 says, "And he had in his right hand seven stars: and out of his mouth went a sharp twoedged sword: and his countenance was as the sun shineth in his strength." And Revelation 19:15 & 21 say, "And out of his mouth goeth a sharp sword, that with it he should smite the nations: and he shall rule them with a rod of iron: and he treadeth the winepress of the fierceness and wrath of Almighty God... And the remnant were slain with the sword of him that sat upon the horse, which sword proceeded out of his mouth: and all the fowls were filled with their flesh."

I do not believe the sword that is mentioned here is a literal sword; I believe it is the Word of God. Ephesians 6:17 says, "And take the helmet of salvation, and the sword of the Spirit, which is the word of God:"

Nearly six thousand years ago God said, "let there be", and there was! When Christ looks down on this vast army gathered together, He'll simply say, "Let there be defeat", and there will be!

John 18:1-6 is a typology of this probability, "When Jesus had spoken these words, he went forth with his disciples over the brook Cedron, where was a garden, into the which he entered, and his disciples. And Judas also, which betrayed him, knew the place: for Jesus ofttimes resorted thither with his disciples. Judas then, having received a band of men and officers from the chief priests and Pharisees, cometh thither with lanterns and torches and weapons. Jesus therefore, knowing all things that should come upon him, went forth, and said unto them, Whom seek ye? They answered him, Jesus of Nazareth. Jesus saith unto them, I am he. And Judas also, which betrayed him, stood with them. As soon then as he had said unto them, I am he, they went backward, and fell to the ground."

When the army is gathered together at Armageddon, and Jesus Christ speaks, as the "sword" (Word) proceeds out of His mouth, with a thunderous voice, and lightning, and smoke; those people will be so confused, that undoubtedly, they will turn against one another, just like the armies did that came against Jehoshaphat, at the end of 2 Chronicles, chapter 20.

Here's a better, Scriptural picture of it in Zechariah 12:1-4, "The burden of the word of the Lord for Israel, saith the Lord, which stretcheth forth the heavens, and layeth the foundation of the earth, and formeth the spirit of man within him. Behold, I will make Jerusalem a cup of trembling unto all the people round about, when they shall be in the siege both against Judah and against Jerusalem. And in that day will I make Jerusalem a burdensome stone for all people: all that burden themselves with it shall be cut in pieces, though all the people of the earth be gathered together against it. In that day, saith the Lord, I will smite every horse with astonishment, and his rider with madness: and I will open mine eyes upon the house of Judah, and will smite every horse of the people with blindness."

How will the horses be blinded? Through the brightness of His countenance. Second Thessalonians 2:8 says, "And then shall that Wicked be revealed, whom the Lord shall consume with the spirit of his mouth, and shall destroy with the brightness of his coming".

This battle is going to be over before quick, in a New York minute. Can you imagine the picture? Here's what will happen to those who have gathered together to go to Edom (Petra) to kill the Jews:

    A. The blood will run bridle deep to a horse, in an area approximately 160 miles long, and 20 to 50 miles wide. (See Revelation 14:14-20)

    B. All of the dead rotting bodies will become a feast for the birds. (See Revelation 19: 17, 18, and 21)

    C. The Beast and the False Prophet will be cast alive into the Lake of Fire. (See Revelation 19:20)

What an awesome day that is going to be, for the Christians, the Jews, and the Kingdom of God.

This brings us to the sixth part of our outline regarding the Second Coming. There is much confusion in the interpretation of this judgment, because there are many unfamiliar Greek words used here. When we look at Matthew 25:31-46, please notice that the phrase "all nations" used in verse 32 actually infers "living and dead". The Bible teaches that more is required of those in leadership. Accordingly, I believe the living and the dead rulers of the nations that opposed Israel will be judged here.

    6. The Dividing (Judgment) of the Nations

Matthew 25:31-46, says, "When the Son of man shall come in his glory, and all the holy angels with him, then shall he sit upon the throne of his glory: And before him shall be gathered all nations: and he shall separate them one from another, as a shepherd divideth his sheep from the goats: And he shall set the sheep on his right hand, but the goats on the left. Then shall the King say unto them on his right hand, Come, ye blessed of my father, inherit the kingdom prepared for you from the foundation of the world: For I was an hungred, and ye gave me meat: I was thirsty, and ye gave me drink: I was a stranger, and ye took me in: Naked, and ye clothed me: I was sick, and ye visited me: I was in prison, and ye came unto me. Then shall the righteous answer him, saying, Lord, when saw we thee an hungred, and fed thee? Or thirsty, and gave thee drink? When saw we thee a stranger, and took thee in? or naked, and clothed thee? Or when saw we thee sick, or in prison, and came unto thee? And the King shall answer and say unto them, Verily I say unto you, Inasmuch as ye have done it unto one of the least of these my brethren, ye have done it unto me. Then shall he say also unto them on the left hand, Depart from me, ye cursed into everlasting fire, prepared for the devil and his angels: For I was an hungred, and ye gave me no meat: I was thirsty, and ye gave me no drink: I was a stranger, and ye took me not in: naked, and ye clothed me not, sick, and in prison, and ye visited me not. Then shall they also answer him, saying, Lord, when saw we thee an hungred, or athirst, or a stranger, or naked, or sick, or in prison, and did not minister unto thee? Then shall he answer them, saying, Verily I say unto you, Inasmuch as ye did it not to one of the least of these, ye did it not to me. And these shall go away into everlasting punishment: but the righteous into life eternal."

Some have tried to say this is the same as the Great White Throne Judgment. It is not. This judgment takes place right here on earth. Again, notice the statements, (verse 31) "When the Son of man shall come..." (the Second Coming); and, (verse 32) "Before him shall be gathered all nations...".

Those people (by nation, including those who have survived the Great Tribulation) will be brought before Christ at this judgment. Those who have received the Mark of the Beast, will then (as a result of this judgment), be cast into the Lake of Fire (Matt. 25:41). That's why I believe it will be limited to the leadership, they apparently will not stand before Jesus at the Great White Throne Judgment.

Those who did not receive the Mark of the Beast will be allowed to enter into the Millennial Reign. Matthew 25:34 says they will "inherit the 'kingdom'", which is interpreted, His rule, and His reign.

Remember, these people, who enter the Millennial Reign, do so in their natural, physical bodies (their flesh and bones, earthly body.) They "endured" the Great Tribulation, and were not previously raptured. We, who were raptured, and returned with Christ, will be in our new Glorified Bodies.

Let's continue:

7. Judgment of the Fallen Angels

First Corinthians 6:3 says, "Know ye not that we shall judge angels? How much more things that pertain to this life?

The time of this event, this judgment, is never recorded in the Bible. However, since we will not have any issues with demons (fallen angels) during the Millennial Reign, it just makes sense to me that following the Great Tribulation, before the Millennial Reign begins, will be a natural time for this judgment. There is not anything else said of this, so I won't speculate any further.

Now, this is actually still in the Dispensation of Grace, the Millennial Reign has not yet actually begun.

So, let's answer the question, "How long will all this take?

    a. For Christ, and us, to return
    b. To deliver the Jews in Petra
    c. To defeat the armies at Armageddon
    d. To Judge the Nations, and
    e. To Judge the Fallen Angels?

Is the Bible specific in answering this question? I think so. Daniel 12:11 & 12 says, "And from the time that the daily sacrifice shall be taken away, and the abomination that maketh desolate set up, there shall be a thousand two hundred and ninety days. Blessed is he that waiteth, and cometh to the thousand three hundred and five and thirty days."

I interpret the 1290 days of verse 11 to be the first-half of the seven year period of the Great Tribulation, and the 1335 days of verse 12 to be the second-half. That would leave a 45 day gap in the middle, from the end of the Great Tribulation to the beginning of the Millennial Reign. Would you agree a 45-day transitional period would be sufficient?

Ray James

Chapter 9

The Millennial Reign

Now, in order to understand, and digest, this 1,000 year period of the Millennial Reign, let's break it down into seven categories:

1. What will the Millennial Reign be like for Satan?
2. What will the Millennial Reign be like for Jesus?
3. What will the Millennial Reign be like for the Saints?
4. What will the Millennial Reign be like for the Survivors?
5. What will the Millennial Reign be like for the Salvaged Earth?
6. What will the Millennial Reign be like for Israel?
7. What will the Millennial Reign be like for the Sanctuary?

There is an enormous amount of scripture regarding the Millennial Reign; however, once again, I will not attempt to include every scripture that talks about this topic. But will attempt to at least adequately answer the questions, "What will it be like…?"

The Second Coming, that we've just looked at, and the events of that transitional period, is the bridge between the worst time (Great Tribulation), and the best time (Millennial Reign) this earth has ever known. The Millennial Reign will be unlike anything that has ever taken place on the face of this earth.

Let's also remember two things:

a. This is not in heaven. This is a time when Jesus Christ will be reigning on earth, and ruling all of the inhabitants of earth, for 1,000 years; and,

b. Even though this is going to be a wonderful time on earth, there will still be some who will try to cause trouble.

Also, understand that when Revelation 21:4 says, "God shall wipe away all tears from their eyes", this has not been fulfilled yet. During the Millennial Reign, there will be periods of sorrow and disappointments.

Even though we Christians have been raptured from this earth, and have been to heaven; and, even though we Christians will have our new Glorified Bodies, it is not until after the Great White Throne Judgment that God will wipe away all tears.

1. What will the Millennial Reign be like for Satan?

The devil has been deceiving people since the Garden of Eden, and he still today goes about "seeking whom he may devour."

But during the Millennial Reign, that will stop.

Revelation 20:1-3 says, "And I saw an angel come down from heaven, having the key of the bottomless pit and a great chain in his hand. And he laid hold of the dragon, that old serpent, which is the Devil, and Satan, and bound him a thousand years, And cast him into the bottomless pit, and shut him up, and set a seal upon him, that he should deceive the nations no more, till the thousand years should be fulfilled: and after that he must be loosed a little season."

He will be chained in the bottomless pit, shut up and sealed, not allowed to deceive anyone for 1,000 years.

The father of all lies, won't be able to spread his lies during this time. But don't get too excited, this won't be the end of Satan; he'll just have a thousand year prison sentence, with a short release afterwards.

I'm sure it will be 1,000 years of great frustration and scheming, as he anticipates his release.

2. What will the Millennial Reign be like for our Savior, Jesus Christ?

This is the time, as the King of kings and Lord of lords, as Christ the Messiah will rule and reign on the earth; and He will rule with all the Saints, from all times, and with the survivors of the Great Tribulation, who have not taken the Mark of the Beast.

A. Jesus will ensure that this is a time of peace. Remember, this is not heaven; nevertheless, there will not be any wars during this time.

Isaiah 2:4 says, "And he shall judge among the nations, and shall rebuke many people: and they shall beat their swords into plowshares, and their spears into pruninghooks: nation shall not lift up sword against nation, neither shall they learn war any more."

See also, Micah 4:3.

We can look further in Isaiah and see the results of not having any more wars. Isaiah 32:17-18 says, "And the work of righteousness shall be peace; and the effect of righteousness quietness and assurance for ever. And my people shall dwell in a peaceable habitation, and in sure dwellings, and in quiet resting places;"

Peace, quiet, resting (calm and security), notice the adjectives used here.

Jesus Christ will not only cause it to be that man will not harm another man; He will also see to it that the wild animals won't hurt man.

Ezekiel 34:25 says, "And I will make with them a covenant of peace, and will cause the evil beasts to cease out of the land: and they shall dwell safely in the wilderness, and sleep in the woods."

When God says peace, quiet, and rest, He means it!

B. Jesus will restore the agricultural conditions of the earth.

Do you remember the devastation that the opening of the seals, blowing of the trumpets, and pouring of the vials (bowls) caused, over the last three and one-half years of the Great Tribulation, and during the 45 day transitional period that followed?

The earth is a mess, and the agricultural condition is terrible, following a nuclear war, and chemical war, that has caused catastrophic damage; and Christ will clean it up.

How? Isaiah 2:4 and Micah 4:3 told us "…they shall beat their swords into plowshares, and their spears into pruninghooks (rakes and shovels)…"

As a result, every nation will redirect their military budgets to their agricultural budgets. "They won't make war anymore." The military services will be dissolved.

Should you inquire of GlobalFirePower.com, you will see that over 20 Trillion dollars is being spent by the top 137 nations of the world on defense. Does that give you a better picture of what $20,000,000,000,000 could do to end hunger in every nation around the globe?

Think about that! When the President/Prime Minister/King of the world, Jesus Christ, has just defeated the armies of the world with the "Sword of His mouth" (His Word), why would you need an army, or, better yet, why would you be foolish enough to even want an army?

    C. Jesus will make sure that comfort will be provided for everyone.

Isaiah 12:1 says, "And in that day thou shalt say, O Lord, I will praise thee: though thou wast angry with me, thine anger is turned away, and thou comfortedst me."

And, Isaiah 51:3 says, "For the Lord shall comfort Zion: he will comfort all her waste places; and he will make her wilderness like Eden, and her desert like the garden of the Lord; joy and gladness shall be found therein, thanksgiving, and the voice of melody."

Typically, the best way to bring comfort to someone, is to change their environment. Several years ago my wife and I decided to celebrate our 25th wedding anniversary with a trip to Oahu, Hawaii. Just a short walk away from our hotel we found a little outdoor restaurant, one-half a block off of Waikiki Beach, in Honolulu.

It was a garden of fruit trees, palm trees, flowers and ferns. Even I thought it was absolutely gorgeous. Add to that a warm (not hot) tropical breeze and a great meal. Without a doubt, I was comfortable! After that, we enjoyed a smoothie made of ice cold fresh puréed fruit. I'll have to admit, my comfort meter was pegged out!

Well, according to Isaiah 51:3 that is exactly what God is going to do for Israel. He will take away her rocky, barren, desolate, desert, and replace it with a garden, like Eden.

D. Jesus will ensure that perfect Justice will be administered to each person.

Isaiah 9:7 says, "Of the increase of his government and peace there shall be no end, upon the throne of David, and upon his kingdom, to order it, and to establish it with judgment and with justice from henceforth even for ever. The zeal of the Lord of hosts will perform this."

The innocent will not suffer unjustly. The guilty will not go free, because of a technicality or loop-hole that their slick attorney found.

During the Millennial Reign, perfect justice will prevail. Keep in mind we're going to have mere humans, in their earthly, physical, carnal bodies living here with us.

E. Jesus will make sure that there will be no sickness and no disease.

Now, remember, there are probably going to be millions of people (possibly a billion) who will enter the Millennial Reign in their natural, physical bodies, having survived the Great Tribulation. But during these thousand years, there will be no sickness, and no death, as a result of disease.

Earlier I wrote there would be no need for a military budget. Well, I believe, according to the following verse, there also won't be a need for health insurance any longer.

Isaiah 65:20 says, "There shall be no more thence an infant of days, nor an old man that hath not filled his days: for the child shall die an hundred years old; but the sinner being an hundred years old shall be accursed."

That seems to strongly suggest there will be no more crib deaths for babies, and no sickness or disease for man. The Good

News Bible translates it as, "100 years old will be considered young."

    F. Jesus will make sure that proper instructions are given to all people.

Remember the capital of the world will be in Jerusalem (Zion), and the King of the world will be Christ; and from His throne He will instruct the world, by the inference of Jeremiah, by His appointment of Pastors (out of his bride).

Jeremiah 3:14 & 15 says, "Turn, O backsliding children, saith the Lord; for I am married unto you: and I will take you one of a city, and two of a family, and I will bring you to Zion: And I will give you pastors according to mine heart, which shall feed you with knowledge and understanding."

And, Micah 4:2 says, "And many nations shall come, and say, Come, and let us go up to the mountain of the Lord, and to the house of the God of Jacob; and he will teach us of his ways, and we will walk in his paths: for the law shall go forth of Zion, and the word of the Lord from Jerusalem."

   3. What will the Millennial Reign be like for the Saints?

    A. According to 1 Thessalonians 4:17, "We shall ever be with the Lord."

    B. The things which applied to Jesus, will also apply to, and affect us:

       1. We will help make sure peace prevails.
       2. We will help make sure perfect justice is administered.
       3. We will help make sure proper instructions are given.
       4. We will help make sure everyone is comfortable.

In other words, "We will reign with Him", to administer the affairs of the world.

Revelation 20:4-6 says, "And I saw thrones, and they sat upon them, and judgment was given unto them: and I saw the souls of them that were beheaded for the witness of Jesus, and for the word of God, and which had not worshipped the beast, neither his image, neither had received his mark upon their foreheads, or in their hands; and they lived and reigned with Christ a thousand years. But the rest of the dead lived not again until the thousand years were finished. This is the first resurrection. Blessed and holy is he that hath part in the first resurrection: on such the second death hath no power, but they shall be priests of God and of Christ, and shall reign with him a thousand years."

Let me also insert here an assortment of other scriptures: 2 Timothy 2:11 & 12, "It is a faithful saying: For if we be dead with him, we shall also live with him: If we suffer, we shall also reign with him: if we deny him, he also will deny us:" Revelation 3:21, "To him that overcometh will I grant to sit with me in my throne, even as I also overcame, and am set down with my Father in his throne." Revelation 2:26 & 27, "And he that overcometh, and keepeth my works unto the end, to him will I give power over the nations: And he shall rule them with a rod of iron; as the vessels of a potter shall they be broken to shivers: even as I received of my Father."

Remember, the people we will assist Christ in ruling over, will be those that survived and, those who were born during and after the Great Tribulation.

C. We are going to worship Christ.

Isaiah 66:23 says, "And it shall come to pass, that from one new moon to another, and from one sabbath to another, shall all flesh come to worship before me, saith the Lord."

And, Zechariah 14:16 says, "And it shall come to pass, that every one that is left of all the nations which came against Jerusalem shall even go up from year to year to worship the King, the Lord of hosts, and to keep the feast of the tabernacles."

4. What will the Millennial Reign be like for the Survivors?

Those who survived the Great Tribulation will enter the Millennial Reign in their natural, physical bodies.

A. They will continue to reproduce.

Ezekiel 47:21-23 says, "So shall ye divide this land unto you according to the tribes of Israel. And it shall come to pass, that ye shall divide it by lot for an inheritance unto you, and to the strangers that sojourn among you, which shall beget children among you: and they shall be unto you as born in the country among the children of Israel; they shall have inheritance with you among the tribes of Israel. And it shall come to pass, that in what tribe the stranger sojourneth, there shall ye give him his inheritance, saith the Lord God."

Remember, once before the "survivors" were called "strangers". They are of a different culture and different society. Also remember, during the Millennial Reign there will be no sickness and no disease. Accordingly, wouldn't you also suppose the years of pregnancy and childbirth could then extend far beyond today's years of menopause?

Personally, during this time, I believe it will be possible to see great-grandmothers having babies at the same time as their great-granddaughter's. Remember, in Revelation 20:8, John saw the survivors numbering "as the sand of the sea". (Certainly that is far beyond a few billion.)

B. They will suffer punishment (for disobedience).

Even though Satan will be gone, "bound and cast into the bottomless pit" for 1,000 years (Rev. 20:1-3); the Great Tribulation survivors, and their children, and children's children..., will still have a "sin nature". You don't have to teach a child how to sin; the sin nature is still within the carnal nature of these survivors.

Once again remembering the Bible is filled with metaphors, typologies, and symbolisms; consider with me that Jeremiah, chapter 30, is symbolic of this period of the Millennial Reign. The "rest and quiet" of verse 10 is the same phrase that we have previously looked at in Isaiah 32:17 & 18, describing the Millennial Reign. (To date, Israel has not known rest and quite.)

Accordingly, to ensure this period of "rest and quite", those survivors who oppress Israel will have to be punished.

We earlier entertained the idea that people would not die during the Millennial Reign; as the result of sickness and disease. The punishment of Jeremiah 30:20 (where Jesus will punish all that oppress Israel) will undoubtedly be of varying degrees, up to and including the death penalty.

To illustrate, Isaiah 66:22-24 says, "For as the new heavens and the new earth, which I will make, shall remain before me, saith the Lord, so shall your seed and your name remain. And it shall come to pass, that from one new moon to another, and from one sabbath to another, shall all flesh come to worship before me, saith the Lord. And they shall go forth, and look upon the carcasses of the men that have transgressed against me: for their worm shall not die, neither shall their fire be quenched; and they shall be an abhorring unto all flesh."

C. They will labor.

Isaiah 65:21-23 says, "And they shall build houses, and inhabit them; and they shall plant vineyards, and eat the fruit of them. They shall not build, and another inhabit; they shall not plant, and another eat: for as the days of a tree are the days of my people, and mine elect shall long enjoy the work of their hands. They shall not labour in vain, nor bring forth for trouble; for they are the seed of the blessed of the Lord, and their offspring with them."

Industry, farming, manufacturing, will still be needed, and the survivors and their children, will be the ones to produce this labor.

Remember, those who returned to earth with Jesus, following the Great Tribulation, will be ruling and reigning with Him; administering peace, comfort, justice, and so forth.

    D.   They will be prosperous.

Ezekiel 36:29 – 38 says, "I will also save you from all your uncleannesses: and I will call for the corn, and will increase it, and lay no famine upon you. And I will multiply the fruit of the tree, and the increase of the field, that ye shall receive no more reproach of famine among the heathen. Then shall ye remember your own evil ways, and your doings that were not good, and shall lothe yourselves in your own sight for your iniquities and for your abominations. Not for your sakes do this, saith the Lord God, be it known unto you: be ashamed and confounded for your own ways, O house of Israel. Thus saith the Lord God; In the day that I shall have cleansed you from all your iniquities I will also cause you to dwell in the cities, and the wastes shall be builded. And the desolate land shall be tilled, whereas it lay desolate in the sight of all that passed by. And they shall say, This land that was desolate is become like the garden of Eden; and the waste and desolate and ruined cities are become fenced, and are inhabited. Then the heathen that are left round about you shall know that I the Lord build the ruined places, and plant that that was desolate: I the Lord have spoken it, and I will do it. Thus saith the Lord God; I will yet for this be enquired of by the house of Israel, to do it for them; I will increase them with men like a flock. As the holy flock, as the flock of Jerusalem in her solemn feasts; so shall the waste cities be filled with flocks of men: and they shall know that I am the Lord."

No poor, no hungry, no homeless; all needs met: that's prosperity!

E. They all will speak one language.

Today's language barriers cause a tremendous breakdown in communication; and that won't happen during the Millennial Reign.

Zephaniah 3:9 says, "For then will I turn to the people a pure language, that they may all call upon the name of the Lord, to serve him with one consent."

Will the final earthquake reunite the landmasses of the world? (Remember the mountains are already removed and islands have disappeared.)

5. What will the Millennial Reign be like for the Salvaged Earth?

Remember during the last three and one-half years, during the second half of the Great Tribulation, the earth has suffered tremendous devastation from nuclear, biological and chemical warfare; along with the fire that has fallen from heaven and one-hundred pound hail stones.

Let's briefly refresh our memories:

2nd Seal - War, and global destruction.

3rd Seal - Famine and earth dried up. A day's wages to buy a quart of wheat.

4th Seal - Catastrophic diseases, where one-fourth of the population dies.

6th Seal   - A tremendous earthquake, and stars fall to the earth.

1st Trumpet - Hail, Fire, and Blood rain, and one-third of the trees are burnt up.

2nd Trumpet - The mountains crumble into the sea, and one-third of the sea becomes blood.

3rd Trumpet - One-third part of the rivers (fresh water) are contaminated.

6th Trumpet - One-third of a 200,000,000 man army are slain.

2nd Vial   - The entire sea becomes blood.

3rd Vial   - All remaining fresh water becomes blood.

4th Vial   - Fire is poured out to scorch men.

5th Vial   - Darkness and Pain.

6th Vial   - The Euphrates River is dried up, causing a loss of irrigation and a means for armies to cross.

7th Vial   - A great earthquake, "such as was not since men were upon the earth".

And remember the earthquake that followed, at the Second Coming.

Have you got the picture?

The earth will suffer greatly during the Great Tribulation.

Of course the earth has been declining ever since Adam and Eve sinned, in the Garden of Eden.

Genesis 3:17 & 18 says, "And unto Adam he said, Because thou hast hearkened unto the voice of thy wife, and hast eaten of the tree, of which I commanded thee, saying, Thou shalt not eat of it: cursed is the ground for thy sake; in sorrow shalt thou eat of it all the days of thy life; Thornes also and thistles shall it bring forth to thee; and thou shalt eat the herb of the field:"

And because the ground is cursed, every year it loses more and more of its natural nutrients.

Before the fall of man the rose bushes didn't have thorns, and gardens didn't have weeds.

So, what will the Millennial Reign be like for the Salvaged Earth?

    A. The earth will be restored and the original curse will be lifted.

Amos 9:13 says, "Behold, the days come, saith the Lord, that the plowman shall overtake the reaper, and the treader of grapes him that soweth seed; and the mountains shall drop sweet wine, and all the hills shall melt."

The crops will not have all been harvested, before it's time to replant. There will be a surplus of grapes, and apparently everything else, from season to season; and, I believe it will be the most bountiful harvest ever seen, all without chemicals and fertilizers.

God is going to remove the curse from the ground!

    B. The animal life will be changed.

Isaiah 11:6-9 says, "The wolf also shall dwell with the lamb, and the leopard shall lie down with the kid; and the calf and the young lion and the fatling together; and a little child shall lead them. And the cow and the bear shall feed; their young ones shall lie down together: and the lion shall eat straw like the ox. And the sucking child shall play on the hole of the asp, and the weaned child shall put his hand on the cockatrice' den. They shall not hurt nor destroy in all my holy mountain: for the earth shall be full of the knowledge of the Lord, as the waters cover the sea."

It is my belief that all carnivorous animals will become vegetarians, suggested by verse 7, "…the lion shall eat straw…". Also, I further believe we will all be vegetarians, and animals will no longer be slaughtered for eating. Remember it wasn't until after the curse that God instructed man to eat animals. In the Garden of Eden He said, "Of every tree of the garden thou may freely eat."

Isaiah, chapter 11, seems to infer the wild nature of animals will be taken away during the Millennial Reign and we will once again be able to tell the animals what to do, as God originally gave man dominion over them.

6. What will the Millennial Reign be like for Saved Israel?

Remember, Israel has been, and still is God's chosen people.

It appears to me, that during the Millennial Reign the Jews will occupy a different status, or relationship, to God.

A. They will be restored to their first relationship with God. Isaiah 62:1-5 says, "For Zion's sake will I not hold my peace, and for Jerusalem's sake I will not rest, until the righteousness thereof go forth as brightness, and the salvation thereof as a lamp that burneth. And the Gentiles shall see thy righteousness, and all kings thy glory: and thou shalt be called by a new name, which the mouth of the Lord shall name. Thou shalt also be a crown of glory in the hand of the Lord, and a royal

> diadem in the hand of thy God. Thou shalt no more be termed Forsaken; neither shall thy land any more be termed Desolate: but thou shalt be called Hephzibah, and thy land Beulah: for the Lord delighteth in thee, and thy land shall be married. For as a young man marrieth a virgin, so shall thy sons marry thee: and as the bridegroom rejoiceth over the bride, so shall thy God rejoice over thee."

No longer will the Jews be persecuted, just because they are Jews. Hephzibah, is defined as "my delight" [is found in her].

Many times in Scripture God refers to Israel as being unfaithful, because they turned to worship Baal, and so forth. During the Millennial Reign Israel will be referred to as faithful, and, the one that is true to God.

> B. Israel will be exalted before the Gentiles. Again, Isaiah 62:2 says, "And the Gentiles shall see thy righteousness, and all kings thy glory: and thou shalt be called by a new name, which the mouth of the Lord shall name."

Now, again, remember, we are referring to the "survivors", so we have to separate them into two groups: Gentiles and Jews.

Speaking to the Jews, God says to them (Isaiah 49:22 & 23), "Thus saith the Lord God, Behold, I will lift up mine hand to the Gentiles, and set up my standard to the people: and they shall bring thy sons in their arms, and thy daughters shall be carried upon their shoulders. And kings shall be thy nursing fathers, and their queens thy nursing mothers: they shall bow down to thee with their face toward the earth, and lick up the dust of thy feet; and thou shalt know that I am the Lord: for they shall not be ashamed that wait for me."

It appears as if God will cause the surviving Gentiles to be the servants of the Jews.

C. Israel will become God's witness during the Millennial Reign.

Zephaniah 3:20 says, "At that time will I bring you again, even in the time that I gather you: for I will make you a name and a praise among all people of the earth, when I turn back your captivity before your eyes, saith the Lord."

The Jews, who survived the Great Tribulation, and did not take the Mark of the Beast, who are allowed to enter the Millennial Reign, are going to occupy a higher status than the surviving Gentiles.

7. What will the Millennial Reign be like for the Sanctuary?

We have already briefly considered the fact that we will worship God; but the place of worship, and the method of worship will be different.

A. Because the temple will again be present in the Millennial Reign.

Remember, the temple has been rebuilt, and the Antichrist has gone into it and sat on the throne (the Abomination of Desolation). As a result of this desecration it will either be cleansed or rebuilt. But one thing is for sure: There will be a temple.

Isaiah 2:3 says, "And many people shall go and say, Come ye, and let us go up to the mountain of the Lord, to the house of the God of Jacob; and he will teach us of his ways, and we will walk in his paths: for out of Zion shall go forth the law, and the word of the Lord from Jerusalem."

Ezekiel, chapters 40-48 (nine chapters), describe this new temple in detail, and I would encourage you to read it.

B. Sacrifices will again take place.

Isaiah 56:5-7 says, "Even unto them will I give in mine house and within my walls a place and a name better than of sons and of daughters: I will give them an everlasting name, that shall not be cut off. Also the sons of the stranger, that join themselves to the Lord, to serve him, and to love the name of the Lord, to be his servants, every one that keepeth the sabbath from polluting it, and taketh hold of my covenant; Even them will I bring to my holy mountain, and make them joyful in my house of prayer: their burnt offerings and their sacrifices shall be accepted upon mine altar; for mine house shall be called an house of prayer for all people."

There are some theologians who believe that these sacrifices will be made in order to teach the children being born during the Millennial Reign about how Jesus, their Messiah, shed His blood for them. The blood of these animals will not save them, or atone for their sins, but will be used to teach them what Jesus Christ did for them; and, these children will have to believe what is taught, in order for them to go to heaven.

Chapter 10

Satan's Last Stand

At the beginning of the Millennial Reign Satan was given a "Prison Sentence" of 1,000 years, and was cast into the bottomless pit.

Revelation 20:1-3 says, "And I saw an angel come down from heaven, having the key of the bottomless pit and a great chain in his hand. And he laid hold on the dragon, that old serpent, which is the Devil, and Satan, and bound him a thousand years, And cast him into the bottomless pit, and shut him up, and set a seal upon him, that he should deceive the nations no more, till the thousand years should be fulfilled: and after that he must be loosed a little season."

At this point we are considering a brief period here, "a little season", that is between the Millennial Reign and the Great White Throne Judgment.

Let's look at it in four segments:

1. The Release
2. The Reasons
3. The Revolt
4. The Results

Everything God has ever done, and will do, has a reason. He is a God of plan and purpose, not a fickle God Who changes His mind on a whim, like some of us.

1. The Release

The chains will be removed, and Satan will come up out of the bottomless pit, and he will set out again to lie and deceive. He will do the only thing he knows to do, lie and deceive, as he has always done.

Revelation 20:7-10 says, "And when the thousand years are expired, Satan shall be loosed out of his prison, And shall go out to deceive the nations which are in the four quarters of the earth, Gog, and Magog, to gather them together to battle: the number of whom is as the sand of the sea. And they went up on the breadth of the earth, and compassed the camp of the saints about, and the beloved city: and fire came down from God out of heaven, and devoured them. And the devil that deceived them was cast into the lake of fire and brimstone, where the beast and false prophet are, and shall be tormented day and night for ever and ever."

One thousand years is not going to change Satan. When he comes out of the bottomless pit he knows he has a very short time, and he is going to be more vicious than he has ever been before.

How much time will he have? Revelation 20:3 said he has "a little season". Typically, when the Bible refers to a "season" it is approximately equivalent to a three month period. We may not know the exact number of days, but we do know it will be long enough for him to travel to the four quarters of the earth to gather together an army, to battle against Jesus Christ.

Remember, Satan is not omnipresent, so this will take a little time, and I have a feeling he may not trust this task to other demons; he will probably want to do this (last deception) himself. What's the old saying, "If you want something done right, do it yourself."

2. The Reason

Remember, the "Millennial Kingdom Children", those who did not take the Mark of the Beast, and who have now accepted Jesus as their Lord and Savior, have not put on their Glorified Body.

They, and those who have been born during the Millennial Reign, still have a sinful nature. One thousand years of peace, and living under the reign of King Jesus will not erase that nature. Man's heart will still be wicked, that's simply a by-product of sin.

Another reason to consider is simply because God has given every person the will to make a choice. We are all free moral agents. From eternity past God has always given us a choice.

Let's put this into perspective. Sacrifices have been made, and the "Kingdom Children" have been taught about the salvation plan of Jesus Christ; but Satan has not been able to offer them an alternative.

Yes, they have seen the consequences of not serving God, as a result of the death penalty, but they have not actually been given a choice, through the lies and deception of Satan.

Let me illustrate it this way: you cannot choose white until you see black, or any other color for comparison.

Satan will be loosed to give them a choice.

How many "Kingdom Children" are we talking about? Hundreds of thousands would be too low of a number. Probably tens of millions and some believe billions; as mothers, grandmothers, great-grandmothers, great-great-grandmothers continue to have babies. Think about it, who wouldn't want to have children in a perfect world, of the Millennial Reign.

Above in Revelation 20:8, the phrase was made, "…the number of whom is as the sand of the sea."

Consider also, the only reason many, and probably most, of these "Kingdom Kids" have followed Jesus, is because of fear of punishment, incited by the public display of the burning bodies (with worms), laying in the streets.

But now, through deceitful lies, they will be given a choice, which will (for some) negate their fear (just like today).

Bottom line: These kids, some hundreds of years old, will not be able to make it to heaven without making a choice to accept what Jesus did for them at Calvary.

It's just like for us today. God never jerked your legs out from under you and made you fall down on your knees and repent of your sins… you made a choice!

3. The Revolt

I believe Satan's influence is going to spread like wild-fire, and many will choose to follow him.

Men and women, boys and girls, who have lived hundreds of years in a Garden of Eden type of environment, under the perfect rule of Jesus Christ, will choose to turn against God. I can hardly fathom that, but, then, it's difficult to understand why so many follow Satan today.

Then, Satan will form an army, of these kingdom kids, and he will try to overthrow the rule of Jesus Christ. How? Probably as simple as when he deceived Eve in the original Garden, when he said, "do you really believe God would…?)

Which brings us to the fourth part:

4. The Results

Simple. Total and complete victory for the saints; that's one thing that never changes.

Revelation 20:9 says, "…and fire came down from God out of heaven, and devoured them", and all that followed Satan will perish, during this final war.

Another result: (vs 10) "The devil that deceived them was cast into the lake of fire and brimstone…" to be tormented day and night for ever and forever; every minute and every second of every day, without time off or vacation, forever!

Chapter 11

The Great White Throne Judgment

There are some, for various reasons, who have erroneously been taught that there is one general judgment, at the end of time, where Jesus will say to those gathered (in a "Heaven's Gates and Hell's Flames" manner), "you can go to heaven, and you can't".

Actually, the Great White Throne Judgment will be the fourth judgment that we have looked at: The Judgment Seat of Christ (Bema Judgment) where Christians will stand and receive rewards; The Judgment of Fallen Angels; and The Judgment of the Nations.

Let's break down the Great White Throne Judgment like this:

1. The Judge of the Throne
2. The Journey to the Throne
3. The Jury of the Throne
4. The Judged of the Throne
5. The Judgment of the Throne
6. The Just of the Throne

This judgment will be held at the end of the Millennial Reign, but before the New Heaven and New Earth, and before Jesus "wipes away all tears".

This is the only judgment where every person who has ever been born on planet Earth will be present.

I didn't say "will be judged", but I believe will be present.

Now, let's read Revelation 20:11-15 which says, "And I saw a great white throne, and him that sat on it, from whose face the earth and the heaven fled away; and there was found no place for them. And I saw the dead, small and great, stand before God; and the books were opened: and another book was opened, which is the book of life: and the dead were judged out of those things which were written in the books, according to their works. And the sea gave up the dead which were in it; and death and hell delivered up the dead which were in them: and they were judged every man according to their works. And death and hell were cast into the lake of fire. This is the second death. And whosoever was not found written in the book of life was cast into the lake of fire."

Let's also look at Daniel 7: 9 & 10, which says, "I beheld till the thrones were cast down, and the Ancient of days did sit, whose garment was white as snow, and the hair of his head like the pure wool: his throne was like the fiery flame, and his wheels as burning fire. A fiery stream issued and came forth from before him: thousand thousands ministered unto him, and ten thousand times ten thousand stood before him: the judgment was set, and the books were opened."

What do you hear? I hear millions of saints worshipping God, and then falling silent, as they await His voice. I hear a few of those waiting to be judged quietly whimpering, and then wailing loudly in unison, as they recognize what is about to happen; and then one-by-one the Judge opens the books…

1. The Judge of the Throne

Who is this Judge? Daniel calls Him, "The Ancient of Days"; Who is our Lord and Savior, Jesus, the Christ.

Some would question this, because Revelation 20:12 says, "And I saw the dead, small and great, stand before God, and the books were opened…".

Some interpret this as, God the Father (Eloim, Adonai). But it can't be. It is God the Son, according to John 5:22, which says, "For the Father judgeth no man, but hath committed all judgment unto the Son:"

John 5:27 says, "And hath given him authority to execute judgment also, because he is the Son of man."

The disciple Luke wrote in Acts 10:40-42, "Him God raised up on the third day, and showed Him openly, not to all people, but to witnesses chosen before by God, even to us who ate and drank with Him after He arose from them dead. And He commanded us to preach to the people, and to testify that it is He who was ordained by God to be Judge of the living and the dead." (NKJV)

Then, the Apostle Paul wrote in 2 Timothy 4:1, "I charge thee therefore before God, and the Lord Jesus Christ, who shall judge the quick and the dead at his appearing and his kingdom".

Let there be no doubt, Jesus Christ, the One who gave Himself for us, will be the Judge of the Throne.

2. The Journey to the Throne

Again, I believe every man and woman, and every boy and girl conceived on earth, will be there. This will be the only judgment where every person ever born will be present.

Here are my thoughts: we, as believers, will only be spectators; because we have already been "judged" at the Judgment Seat of Christ. (So we won't be there to be judged.)

The journey to this Throne will come from every imaginable place, from all four corners of the earth, from all time dating back to Adam and Eve, from the grave; even from the pits of hell, Abraham's Bosom and the Abyss. From all time, and every place, man will be released to go to this Judgment.

The first part of Revelation 20:13 says, "And the sea gave up the dead which were in it; and death and hell delivered up the dead which were in them".

Obviously, no sinner will escape. Every man from every age and dispensation will one day ultimately make the pilgrimage to this place.

3. The Jury of the Throne

Let's look again at Revelation 20:12, "And I saw the dead, small and great, stand before God; and the books were opened: and another book was opened, which is the book of life: and the dead were judged out of those things which were written in the books, according to their works."

"Books" (plural) were opened; and another book (singular) was opened, which is the Book of Life.

"Judged out of those things which were written in the books, according to their works."

Some believe these books are each individual's record book, but I don't think so. There is no Scriptural substantiation to support that thought.

So then, what are these books? Does the Word of God tell us? I think so. As a matter of fact, I believe the Word of God describes five books that God is using to record the actions of our lives, in addition to the Book of Life. It is a Jury's duty to hand down a decision, based on evidence; so, what is this evidence, and what are these books?

A. The Book of Conscience.

Look at the words of the Apostle Paul found in Romans 2:14-16, "When outsiders who have never heard of God's law follow it more or less by instinct, they confirm its truth by their obedience. They show that God's law is not something alien, imposed on us from without, but woven into the very fabric of our creation. There is something deep within them that echoes God's yes and no, right and wrong. Their response to God's yes and no will become public knowledge on the day God makes his final decision about every man and woman. The Message from God that I proclaim through Jesus Christ takes into account all these differences." (MSG)

God has placed within us a conscience that is able to discern between right and wrong. When we violate that conscience, "woven into the very fabric of our creation", and do what we know to be wrong, I believe God makes a note of that. Not for Him, but for us to see the proof of the evidence.

B. The Book of Words

Matthew 12:36 & 37 says, "But I say unto you, That every idle word that men shall speak, they shall give account thereof in the day of judgment. For by thy words thou shalt be justified, and by thy words thou shalt be condemned."

If man will give an account of his words, then obviously they must be recorded; and Matthew tells us that He's keeping a record of "every idle word". "Careless words" in the Contemporary English Version and "useless words" in the Good News translation.

Gossip, Back-biting, Complaining, Ridicule, Mud-slinging... should I go on? You get the picture. These words are being recorded, according to Matthew.

C. The Book of Secret (versus public) Words and Works

Romans 2:16 says, "In the day when God shall judge the secrets of men by Jesus Christ according to my gospel."

In addition to the violation of conscience, there are "secrets of men".

Ecclesiastes 12:14 says, "For God shall bring every work into judgment, with every secret thing, whether it be good, or whether it be evil."

There is nothing secret to be withheld from God. He knows, He is recording, and, His Son will one day judge.

Bear with me for another minute, and permit me to share a few more Scriptures regarding this truth, that Satan would like to try to deceive us of:

Second Chronicles 16:9 says, "For the eyes of the Lord run to and fro throughout the whole earth, to shew himself strong in the behalf of them whose heart is perfect toward him. Herein thou hast done foolishly: therefore from henceforth thou shalt have wars."

Zechariah 4:10 says, "For who hath despised the day of small things? for they shall rejoice, and shall see the plummet in the hand of Zerubbabel with those seven; they are the eyes of the Lord, which run to and fro through the whole earth."

Proverbs 15:3 says, "The eyes of the Lord are in every place, beholding the evil and the good."

One more, Hebrews 4:13 says, "Neither is there any creature that is not manifest in his sight: but all things are naked and opened unto the eyes of him with whom we have to do."

You may be able to conceal your thoughts, or your words, or your actions from others, but God knows. He's keeping a record, and one day that book too, will be opened.

D. The Book of Public Works

Romans 2:5 & 6 says in the Amplified Version, "But because of your callous stubbornness and unrepentant heart you are [deliberately] storing up wrath for yourself on the day of wrath when God's righteous judgment will be revealed. He will pay back to each person according to his deeds [justly, as his deeds deserve]:"

Second Corinthians 11:15 says, "So why does it seem strange for Satan's servants to pretend to do what is right? Someday they will get exactly what they deserve." (CEV)

Once again, from the Amplified Version, Matthew 16:27 says, "For the Son of Man is going to come in the glory and majesty of His Father with His angels, and then He will repay each one in accordance with what he has done."

Again, obviously, God must be keeping a record of our works, not for Him, but for the benefit of those standing before Him, who will undoubtedly, be foolish enough to challenge Him.

Let's face it, this Judgment is for "all the marbles", and some, probably most, will not "go down without a fight".

I simply cannot imagine someone standing in front of Jesus the Judge, saying, "Oops, you're right, you got me there; I guess it's off to the Lake of Fire I go." No! I have to imagine the screaming, and begging, and pleading, to no avail. It's too late, and the records prove the events of their lives.

E. The Book of Life

Revelation 20:15 says, "And whosoever was not found written in the book of life was cast into the lake of fire."

Literally, the word "life" used here, means: to live, or living. In other words, no longer dead in trespasses and sin.

John the Revelator describes seeing "the holy city, new Jerusalem, coming down from God out of heaven," in Revelation 21:2, and goes on to say, in verse 27, "And there shall in no wise enter into it any thing that defileth, neither whatsoever worketh abomination, or maketh a lie: but they which are written in the Lamb's book of life."

There is no better time than now, to once again bow our head, and pray to God, that if there be anything in our life that is displeasing to Him, to repent of it, and ask Him to forgive us, and cleanse us from all unrighteousness, and then thank Him that we know our name is written in the Lamb's Book of Life.

Repentance is turning away from our old sinful, carnal, selfish ways, and turning to Jesus the Christ, our Lord and Savior; the One Who has already paid the price for our sins, and choosing to live our lives for Him, following Him, to please only Him.

Now, hold on to your Bible, hang on to the cross, and hold fast to your theology, because we are about to look at something you may not have ever considered before, and that is:

4. The Judged of the Throne

Let me just come right out and say it: I believe there will be some Saints who will also be judged at the Great White Throne Judgment, so let me explain why.

Revelation 20:15 says, "And whosoever was not found written in the book of life was cast into the lake of fire."

Can that be interpreted that some could be found in the Book of Life? Sure.

Hebrews 9:27 says, "...it is appointed unto men once to die, but after this the judgment:"

We must remember that many of these people standing at the Great White Throne Judgment came through the Great Tribulation and did not take the Mark of the Beast, plus there will be others who were born during the Millennial Reign; and they will have to be judged, and these five books will be opened to them also.

Nevertheless, the vast majority standing in front of the Judge, Jesus Christ, will be the Lost, Unrepentant, Unsaved, Sinners, whose names will not be found in the Book of Life.

5. The Judgement of the Throne

A ruling must follow a judging: guilty or not guilty. A verdict and decision must be made, and a sentence must be given for the conclusion of the judgement.

Revelation 20:15 describes that sentence for the guilty, "And whosoever was not found written in the book of life was cast into the lake of fire." Verse 14 tells us, "...This is the second death."

Very briefly, we, humans, are comprised of a body, soul, and spirit. The body gives us world-consciousness, the soul gives us self-consciousness, and the spirit gives us God-consciousness.

The "first death" is when our body dies; we have no more use for it since we would be no longer in this world.

For the unrepentant, condemned to the Lake of Fire, their spirit will die; cut off from God and no longer God-conscious. However, their soul (mind, will, emotion, and intellect) will live on, and they will "feel" the horrible effects of their environs: total darkness, deafening screams, unconsuming fire, crawling worms, etc. And while that will certainly be torture, I believe the greatest torture will be the loneliness caused by having their spirit removed. Man's spirit connects him to life, just as an umbilical cord connects a baby to life.

And the judgment of the throne will be an eternal judgment. Matthew 25:46 says, "And these shall go away into everlasting punishment: but the righteous into life eternal."

One is "everlasting" the other is "eternal", both are forever!

6. The Just (saved) of the Throne

What will this Judgment be like for us, those who were raptured to heaven, have put on the new glorified body, and returned to earth to rule and reign with Jesus during the Millennial Reign?

Well, we will see men and women, and boys and girls stand before the Throne, that God had asked us to witness to, but we did not. People we worked with and had opportunities to witness to, but did not. Brothers and sisters, sons and daughters, and other relatives, that we never talked to about God, because we believed a lie from Satan that we would offend them, and they would be forever mad at us.

Whose hands will their blood be on? Ezekiel 3:18 & 19 says, "When I say unto the wicked, Thou shalt surely die; and thou givest him not warning, nor speakest to warn the wicked from his wicked way, to save his life; the same wicked man shall die in his iniquity; but his blood will I require at thine hand. Yet if thou warn the wicked, and he turn not from his wickedness, nor from his wicked way, he shall die in his iniquity; but thou hast delivered thy soul."

I have a mental image of the "Just" sitting in the balcony watching former friends, relatives, business associates, and neighbors whose names were not found in the Book of Life, being condemned to a devil's hell, turn and make eye contact and ask, "Why didn't you warn me, why didn't you make me listen?"

At this point God has not wiped away all tears from our eyes.

Take a minute and meditate on the closing words of this chapter, before continuing to the next chapter. What is God asking of you?

RAY JAMES

Chapter 12

The Eternal State

Over the last couple of chapters we have considered much of the ugliness, devastation, and cruelty still to come: The Great Tribulation, the hardships on the survivors to rebuild during the Millennial Reign, and the heartaches of the Great White Throne Judgment for both the sinners and the saints.

It is now time to turn our attention to the blessedness of heaven, and our eternal future, as God finally wipes away our tears.

Revelation 21:1-2 says, "And I saw a new heaven and a new earth: for the first heaven and the first earth were passed away; and there was no more sea. And I John saw the holy city, New Jerusalem, coming down from God out of heaven, prepared as a bride adorned for her husband."

2 Peter 3:10-13 says, "But the day of the Lord will come as a thief in the night; in the which the heavens shall pass away with a great noise, and the elements shall melt with fervent heat, the earth also and the works that are therein shall be burned up. Seeing then that all these things shall be dissolved, what manner of persons ought ye to be in all holy conversation and godliness, Looking for and hasting unto the coming of the day of God, wherein the heavens being on fire shall be dissolved, and the elements shall melt with fervent heat? Nevertheless we, according to his promise,

look for new heavens and a new earth, wherein dwelleth righteousness."

New heavens, new earth, and a new, holy city, Jerusalem. That makes sense to me, because man has corrupted the old heaven, and old earth, and old city of Jerusalem.

Please consider this with me, and I do not present this to you as a conclusion, but simply present this to provoke thought. Consider this the "Ray James" and not the "King James":

The Bible says this earth is going to melt with a fervent heat, and we are to look for a new heaven and a new earth.

Now, think of this: We are referred to as a "new creature" when we get saved, right? Second Corinthians 5:17 says, "Therefore if any man be in Christ, he is a new creature: old things are passed away; behold, all things are become new." Yet, physically we are the same person, in the same flesh; but we have a new heart (spirit) within us, and a new direction and purpose.

But like it or not, I am the same flesh (body), and you are too.

So, let me ask a question: Can this earth experience a "washing by fire", and become a new earth?

Speaking of the Flood, the Apostle Peter writes (2 Peter 3:6), "Whereby the world that then was, being overflowed with water, perished:" The world that then was, was flooded, and perished.

It wasn't completely eliminated, it was just revitalized; and it became a "new earth" after it was washed by water. Just like you and I became "new creatures" after we were washed by His blood.

Will you agree that the "new earth" can, in fact, appear on this same planet? Before you answer that question, let me give you one more Scripture to ponder. Ecclesiastes 1:4 says, "One generation passeth away, and another generation cometh: but the earth abideth for ever."

I'm thinking it probably won't be a total annihilation of this earth, and a brand new one created, but a "cleansing by fire".

Think about it this way: When you "pass away", do you cease to exist? Absolutely not! According to Genesis 2:7, Man has a body, but man is a living soul (and spirit).

My conclusion is, when the term "pass away" is used in the Bible, it does not necessarily mean to "cease to exist".

Also worth noting is the new heaven and new earth do not come down from heaven, only the New Jerusalem.

Now, let's consider the new earth; what do we know about it?

1. It will have no sea (Rev. 21:1)

This will of course create a great deal more surface area than we have now; however, I believe the absence of water will be because Jesus is the "water of life" (John 4:14, Revelation 21:6, and Revelation 22:1 & 17).

Nevertheless, whether you agree with the "cleansing by fire" philosophy, and an entirely different earth, there is one thing for sure: the new earth will be a paradise!

2. There will be no more hell

As we believe it to be today, in the center of this earth (Hell, Abraham's Bosom, the Abyss, Hades, Lake of Fire).

And remember, death and hell were cast into the Lake of Fire (Rev. 20:14). Matthew 25:30 says, "And cast ye the unprofitable servant into outer darkness: there shall be weeping and gnashing of teeth." I'm guessing as the New Heaven comes down, the Lake of Fire will go up, into one of our mysterious "black holes" that scientists see in space today???

Nonetheless, when death and hell are cast into the Lake of Fire, the Lake of Fire will be far removed.

3. The new earth will have no trace of sin

Isaiah 65:17 says, "For, behold, I create new heavens and a new earth: and the former shall not be remembered, nor come into mind."

Since the original sin in the Garden of Eden, sin has permeated this earth. One day, every trace of that will be removed, and forgotten.

Let's turn our attention to the new heaven. What do we know about it?

Revelation 21:1 says, "And I saw a new heaven and a new earth: for the first heaven and the first earth were passed away; and there was no more sea."

Notice carefully, "the first heaven was passed away". Heaven; singular.

The Bible clearly teaches there are three heavens. (Our immediate atmosphere, outer space, and the location of the Throne of God.)

> A. The first heaven is our atmosphere. Genesis 1:8 says, "And God called the firmament Heaven. And the evening and the morning were the second day."

Daniel 4:12 says, "The leaves thereof were fair, and the fruit thereof much, and in it was meat for all: the beasts of the field had shadow under it, and the fowls of the heaven dwelt in the boughs thereof, and all flesh was fed of it."

The Hebrew words used here for heaven is shaw-mah-yim, meaning "aloft" or "the sky"; or, more literally "the visible arch in which the clouds move".

Ever since the slow destruction of the firmament, caused by sin, our atmosphere has become more and more polluted.

The "new heaven", the first heaven, our atmosphere, will eradicate the pollution from earth's atmosphere.

    B. The second heaven is the space above our atmosphere where the sun, moon, and stars are located.

Genesis 22:17 says, "That in blessing I will bless thee, and in multiplying I will multiply thy seed as the stars of the heaven…" This heaven is our solar system, and location of other galaxies.

The Hebrew word here used for heaven is: shaw-mah´-yin, from sha-meh, meaning "where the celestial bodies revolve".

Psalm 19:1 says, "The heavens declare the glory of God; and the firmament sheweth his handywork."

Heavens, plural… everything we see when we look up, through our atmosphere, and into the second heaven.

    C. The third heaven is the place where God dwells, which is beyond our vision (with or without the Hubble Telescope).

In II Corinthians 12:2 Paul writes, "I knew a man in Christ above fourteen years ago, (whether in the body, I cannot tell; or whether out of the body, I cannot tell: God knoweth;) such an one caught up to the third heaven."

The Greek word used here for heaven, is: oo-ran-os', meaning "elevated", but not just "high" this word implies "eternity": in other words, "elevated farther that we know about".

Okay, we are examining the "new heaven". I believe when John said (Rev. 21:1), "I saw a new heaven…" the new heaven he is referring to is a new atmosphere around the new (fire washed) earth.

I must insert a story I heard years ago, "A little girl was standing with her mother, looking up at the sky one night and commented, "O, mother, if heaven is so beautiful on the wrong side, imagine what it must be like on the right side."

Okay, there will be a new heaven, and a new earth, and there is something in the 3rd Heaven that will come down:

4. Which is called "The New Jerusalem"

But before we look at what the New Jerusalem will have, let's look at what will be missing.

Here it is, wait no longer, Revelation 21:2-4 says, "And I John saw the holy city, new Jerusalem, coming down from God out of heaven, prepared as a bride adorned for her husband. And I heard a great voice out of heaven saying, Behold, the tabernacle of God is with men, and he will dwell with them, and they shall be his people, and God himself shall be with them, and be their God. And God shall wipe away all tears from their eyes; and there shall be no more death, neither sorrow, nor crying, neither shall there be any more pain: for the former things are passed away."

When this New Jerusalem descends, the tears, sorrow, crying, and pain will be wiped away FOREVER!

Permit me to pause again, to put all of this into perspective. We have just witnessed the Great White Throne Judgment, where many of our friends, relatives, former business associates, and neighbors, have been cast into the Lake of Fire, and exiled into outer space.

I believe that at some point while every person that was ever created is assembled in the 3rd Heaven, that God will purify and purge this earth, and the 1st Heaven below.

As soon as the last sinner is sentenced to the Lake of Fire, we are going for another outer space ride, and will again descend from the 3rd Heaven, this time to the new earth, and, possibly, on the New Jerusalem. Then, simultaneously, God will wipe away our tears, and our memories of the past.

When I say "possibly on the New Jerusalem", permit me to qualify that statement. First, the New Jerusalem will be a city of tremendous size; and, second, it is doubtful that you and I will be six foot tall, 200 pound beings.

Revelation 21:16 says, "And the city lieth foursquare, and the length is as large as the breadth: and he measured the city with a reed, twelve thousand furlongs. The length and the breadth and the height of it are equal."

Let's unpack that verse: A furlong is 220 yards, times 3 (to reduce to feet), equals 660 feet. 660 feet times 12,000 furlongs equals 7,920,000 feet, divided by 5280 feet (one mile) equals 1,500 miles, exactly.

The distance from Boston to Miami (north to south) is approximately 1,500 miles. (1,497 miles via I-95)

The distance from Philadelphia to Denver (east to west) is approximately 1,500 miles. (1,574 miles due west, as the eagle flies.)

Cubed! The length, breadth, and height are equal. This is one city!

Now, I don't know if the New Jerusalem will be suspended above the earth, or, if it will rest upon the earth. But I am confident that we will be able to travel to and from any point on earth, to the New Jerusalem.

Interesting to note, Revelation 21:25 says, "And the gates of it shall not be shut at all by day: for there shall be no night there."

The typical, Biblical, interpretation of the phrase, "the gates shall not be shut", means there will be a coming into and a going out of.

When I read the description of the New Heaven, Earth, and Jerusalem, my finite mind has a hard time comprehending it. First Corinthians 2:9 says, "But as it is written, Eye hath not see, nor ear heard, neither have entered into the heart of man, the things which God hath prepared for them that love him."

I like the way Isaiah said it in chapter 64, verse 4, "For since the beginning of the world men have not heard, not perceived by the ear, neither hath the eye seen, O God, beside thee, what he hath prepared for him that waiteth for him."

No matter how much our imagination can ponder the greatness of all this, no doubt it will be even greater!

Now, what will the New Jerusalem have?

A. The New Jerusalem will have very unique foundations.

Revelation 21:19 & 20 says, "And the foundations of the wall of the city were garnished with all manner of precious stones. The first foundation was jasper; the second, sapphire; the third, a chalcedony; the fourth, an emerald; The fifth, sardonyx; the sixth, sardius; the seventh, chrysolyte; the eight, beryl; the ninth, a topaz; the tenth, a chrysoprasus; the eleventh, a jacinth; the twelfth, an amethyst."

What a beautiful rainbow of colors the foundations will be: blue, green, gray, red, violet, and purple.

    B. And notice the walls of Jasper described in Revelation 21:17 & 18, "And he measured the wall thereof, an hundred and forty and four cubits, according to the measure of a man, that is, of the angel. And the building of the wall of it was of jasper: and the city was pure gold, like unto clear glass."

My dictionary tells me jasper is typically red, but can also be found in yellow or brown opaque quartz. Whatever the colors are, above these beautiful foundations, will be equally beautiful walls of jasper.

Now, remember, the walls of a city, especially during the time of John's writing, were for protection. But these 262 foot tall walls, will only be for beauty.

    C. The City will have Pearly Gates.

Revelation 21:12, 13 and 21a says, "And had a wall great and high, and had twelve gates, and at the gates twelve angels, and names written thereon, which are the names of the twelve tribes of the children of Israel: On the east three gates; on the north three gates; on the south three gates; and on the west three gates... And the twelve gates were twelve pearls: every several gate was of one pearl:"

Each gate is not made of pearls, but, rather, each is a singular pearl. (The little boy hiding inside of me wants to ask: cultured or simulated?)

    D. The City will have a golden street.

The rest of verse 21 (above) says, "...and the street of the city was pure gold, as it were transparent glass."

Did you notice that? Street (singular), of gold. We used to sing a song that we would, "walk on streets of gold"; and, my apologies to the song-writer, but I don't believe that's accurate. Verse 21 says, "street" (singular).

A few years ago I was visiting San Francisco, California. Having read about how Lombard Street is supposedly the crookedest street in America, I had to drive over and see it for myself.

I believe the "street of gold" in the New Jerusalem, will probably be a singular "spiral" street that starts at the bottom of the city, and winds its way up through many levels to the top; but notice also, it will be "as it were transparent glass." Only God, the Creator, could design such a street, and I can't wait to see it.

E. The City will have a bright light.

Revelation 21:23 says, "And the city had no need of the sun, neither of the moon, to shine in it: for the glory of God did lighten it, and the Lamb is the light thereof."

Jesus Christ will illuminate the city! This is probably the reason for the transparency in heaven. What do you think? If Christ is omnipresent, the light will radiate from everywhere. No shadows, just light penetrating from every direction.

F. The City will have a pure river, and, a tree of life.

Revelation 22: 1 & 2 says, "And he shewed me a pure river of water of life, clear as crystal, proceeding out of the throne of God and of the Lamb. In the midst of the street of it, and on either side of the river, was there the tree of life, which bare twelve manner of fruits, and yielded her fruit every month: and the leaves of the tree were for the healing of the nations."

Some of the things I love most about the south are the colonial mansions, with the tree-lined drives, forming beautiful canopies across the drives.

Picture this same thing, but put colored fruit on the trees, and change the color every month.

G. A City without a temple.

Revelation 21:22 says, "And I saw no temple therein: for the Lord God Almighty and the Lamb are the temple of it."

A temple is a place where people gather to worship. This city won't need a temple for people to gather in. Why? Because the place where people will gather to worship, will be at the feet of an omnipresent God.

Let me leave you with one additional thought to ponder, about this city, the New Jerusalem. Where is it today?

I believe it is already designed, built, and located in the third heaven. In John 14:2 & 3 Jesus said, "In my Father's house are many mansions: If it were not so, I would have told you. I go to prepare a place for you. And if I go and prepare a place for you, I will come again, and receive you unto myself; that where I am, there ye may be also."

Without a doubt, Jesus is prepared for His Father to instruct Him to call us home. The preparations of these two verses have already been made.

Then following the Great White Throne Judgment, the city, the New Jerusalem will descend from heaven according to Rev. 21:2.

Not only will the Holy City descend from heaven, but God will also vacate the third heaven, and descend with it.

Revelation 21:3 says, "And I heard a great voice out of heaven saying, Behold, the tabernacle of God is with men, and he will dwell with them, and they shall be his people, and God himself shall be with them, and be their God."

Chapter 13

The Final Recorded Words of Christ

What an amazing experience John the Revelator must have had, as the Angel was describing the eschatological events of God's prophetic calendar to him.

And equally wonderful would have been the occasion of John penning the final words of Jesus Christ, found at the end of Revelation 22:

"And, behold, I come quickly; and my reward is with me, to give every man according as his work shall be. I am Alpha and Omega, the beginning and the end, the first and the last. Blessed are they that do his commandments, that they may have right to the tree of life, and may enter in through the gates into the city. For without are dogs, and sorcerers, and whoremongers, and murderers, and idolaters, and whosoever loveth and maketh a lie. I Jesus have sent mine angel to testify unto you these things in the churches. I am the root and the offspring of David, and the bright and morning star. And the Spirit and the bride say, Come. And let him that heareth say, Come. And let him that is athirst come. And whosoever will, let him take the water of life freely. For I testify unto every man that heareth the words of the prophecy of this book, If any man shall add unto these things, God shall add unto him the plagues that are written in this book: And if any man shall take away from the words of the book of this prophecy, God shall take away his part out of the book of life, and out of the holy city, and from the things which are written in this book. He which testifieth these things saith, Surely I come quickly. Amen."

And we say: Even so, come, Lord Jesus.

Early on the morning of February 14, 1987 I was awakened verbally speaking the words of His final invitation, found in verse 17: "And the Spirit and the bride say, Come. And let him that heareth say, Come. And let him that is athirst come. And whosoever will, let him take the water of life freely."

It is my prayer that you too will embrace these words.

Chapter 14

Book Review
The Short Version

1. The next event to be fulfilled on God's prophetic calendar is the Rapture.

   A. What is the Rapture:

   Literally, to be transported from one location to another.

   B. Who will be involved in the Rapture?

   1. Jesus Christ ("For the Lord Himself shall descend..." 1 Thess. 4:16-18)

   2. The Archangel ("with the voice of the archangel" Jude 9 & Dan. 12:1)

   3. Every Christian who has died ("The dead in Christ shall rise first" 1 Cor. 15:52)

   4. Every Christian who is alive ("Then we which are alive and remain shall be caught up together with them in the clouds." 1 Thess. 4:17)

5. Every Child who has not reached the age of accountability.

C. When will the Rapture take place?

Before the Great Tribulation (Rom. 5:9, 1 Thess. 1:10, 1 Thess. 5:9 show us we will be spared from the wrath to come.)

Remember the "church" is mentioned several times in Revelation up to Chapter 6, but in Chapter 6, when the Seals are opened, and the Great Tribulation begins, the church is never mentioned again. That is why I believe in a Pre-Trib Rapture.

D. What will be the results of the Rapture?

1. The Saints will be gone.

2. All Babies and mentally challenged will be gone.

3. An initial time of havoc on earth:

Auto/train/plane crashes; babies disappearing from nurseries and wombs; people missing world-wide, and the list goes on and on.

2. Our New Glorified Bodies

A. It will be like the body of resurrected Jesus (Phil. 3:21, and 1 John 3:2)

B. It will be a body of flesh and bones (Luke 24:39)

C. It will be recognizable (1 Co. 13:12)

D. It will be a body in which the Spirit totally dominates (1 Co. 15:44)

E. It will be unrestricted by time, space, and gravity (Luke 24:31, John 20:19 & 26)

F. It will be an eternal body (2 Cor. 5:1)

G. It will be a glorious body (Dan. 12:2-3, 1 Cor. 15:43, Rom. 8:18)

3. The Judgment Seat of Christ

   A. What is the Judgment Seat of Christ?

   This is the judgment where all believers will stand before Christ and give an account for their stewardship. (Rom. 14:10-12, 1 Cor. 3:11-15, 2 Cor. 5:10)

   Remember, this is the Bema Seat, and only the winners stood before the Bema Seat to receive their rewards.

   B. Who will be involved in the Judgment Seat of Christ?

   1. The Judge, Jesus Christ (John 5:22)

   2. All raptured believers (from time and eternity past, Rom. 14:10)

   C. What will Christ (the Judge) be concerned with at this Judgment?

   1. He will not be concerned with punishing the believers, because our sin has already been dealt with at Calvary, never to be remembered again (He. 8:12 & 10:17)
   2. He will be concerned with:

a. How Christians conducted themselves concerning their stewardship while on earth (1 Peter 4:10, 1 Cor. 4:1 & 2)

   b. How we managed ourselves according to our privileges and responsibilities as Christians.

   c. Why we did what we did (our motives, 1 Cor. 3:13, 1 Cor. 4:5)

   d. Why we didn't do what we should have (James 4:17)

D. What will be the results of the Judgment Seat of Christ?

   1. Some will lose their rewards (1 Cor. 3:15)

   2. Some will not receive every reward Christ had planned for them (1 John 8)

   3. We will receive rewards for what we have done (1 Cor. 3:14)

We considered the 5 Crowns of Reward

1. The Incorruptible Crown (1 Cor. 9:25-27)

   For those who overcome selfish/sinful desires and who kept their flesh under subjection.

2. The Crown of Rejoicing (1 Thess. 2:19 & 20)

   For those who have won others to the Lord.

3. The Crown of Life (Rev. 2:10)

For those who have been heavily persecuted, with intense suffering and trials (martyrs?).

4. The Crown of Righteousness (2 Tim. 4:8)

   Appears to be for those who are looking for and longing for His return.

5. The Crown of Glory (1 Peter 5:2-4)

   For those who have been faithful to study and teach the uncompromising Word of God.

Our crowns will be used to glorify, praise and worship God (Rev. 4:10 & 11)

      E. What are the Results of the Judgment Seat of Christ, that should be present in our lives today?

      We should want to live every day pleasing to God (1 John 2:28).

  4. The Marriage and the Marriage Supper of the Lamb

    A. The Proof of the Marriage (Rom. 7:4, 2 Co. 11:2, Rev. 19:7-9)

    B. The Place of the Marriage

      1. Place in time: following the Judgment Seat of Christ, and before the Second Coming.

      2. Geographical Place: In the Third Heaven; because it is from heaven that we will return to earth at the Second Coming (Rev. 19:11 & 14)

    C. Who are the Participants in this Marriage?

1. God the Father (Host, Luke 14:16-23)

2. The Bride-Groom (Christ, John 3:27-30, Luke 5:32-35)

3. The Bride (Saints, the Church, Eph. 5:22-32, 2 Cor. 11:2)

4. The Invited Guests (Rev. 19:9, John 3:29)

   Some believe these "guests" to be the angels, and some believe they are the Old Testament Saints (Pre-N.T. Church)

D. The Pattern of the Marriage.

  1. The Betrothal

     Be chosen (Eph. 1:3 & 4)

     Payments/Dowry (1 Cor. 6:19-20, 1 Pe. 1:18-19)

  2. The Presentation (Rev. 4:1, Jude 24, 2 Cor. 11:2)

  3. The Celebration (John 2 describes a public marriage celebration)

5. The Great Tribulation

While the saints are in heaven standing before Christ at the Judgment Seat of Christ, then at the Marriage and Marriage Supper of the Lamb; the inhabitants of earth will be experiencing seven years of the Great Tribulation here on earth.

   A. First, we studied the titles of the Great Tribulation:

     1. The Tribulation (Matt. 24:21 & 29)

2. The Day of Trouble (Dan. 12:1)
3. The Overspreading of Abominations (Dan. 9:27)
4. The Indignation (Is. 26:20 & 34:2)
5. The Hour of His Judgment (Rev. 14:7)
6. The Great Day of His Wrath (Rev. 6:17)
7. The Time of the End (Dan. 12:9)
8. The Seventieth Week (Dan. 9:24-27)
9. The Great Day of the Lord (Zeph. 1:14)
10. The Time of Jacob's Trouble (Jer. 30:7)
11. The Day of God's Vengeance (Is. 34:8 & 63:4)

Knowing these titles helps us to keep from confusing them with other events.

B. The Purpose of the Great Tribulation

Everything God does, has a purpose.

1. The primary purpose of the Great Tribulation is to prepare Israel for her Messiah. (Eze. 20:37-38 and Zech. 13:8-9)

Remember the symbolisms and typologies of these Scriptures as you re-read them.

Remember also, during this time Judaism must be abolished, because Christianity cannot dominate a Judaistic world. (Malachi 3:3)

2. Then, the second purpose for the Great Tribulation is to pour out His judgements on the unrighteous. (Ro. 1:18, 2 Thess. 2:8-12, Isaiah 26:20-21)

C. The Mark of the Tribulation, which is the number 666. (Rev. 13:16-18)

Because of its versatility, I believe the bar code will be used for this Mark, which is separated at the beginning, middle, and end with the character of a "6". (Interestingly, today, the first three digits of a bar code denote a country.)

    1. This Mark will invoke God's wrath. (Rev. 16:1-2)

    2. In numerology, "6" is the Biblical number for man; it is an incomplete number.

    3. It will be required if the individual wants to buy/sell/trade anything, and will be placed in the right hand or forehead of the person. (Rev. 13:17)

    4. Once taken it will seal the person's future. (Rev. 14:9-11 & 19:20)

D. The 2 Witnesses of the Great Tribulation (Rev. 11:3)

These 2 Witnesses will preach the gospel message, and will probably be responsible for the salvation of the 144,000 (which we will review next). Then, the 144,000 will scatter throughout the entire world.

For chronology purposes, these 2 Witnesses will appear very soon after the Rapture of the Church.

    1. And, they have a very special power. (Rev. 11:5-6)

    2. They will be the light of Christ on earth. (Rev. 11:4, the key word here is "candlesticks". Incidentally, to consider the 2 olive trees of verse 4, look at Zechariah, chapter 4.)

3. They will have a limited time on earth. (Rev. 11:3 & 7)

4. Then, because of the deception by Satan, they will receive no further respect. (Rev. 11:8-10)

5. They will be killed. (Rev. 11:7-8)

6. And, after three and one-half days, SURPRISE!!! (Rev. 11:11-12)

E. The 144,000 of the Great Tribulation (Rev. 7:1-4)

Who are they? Jews! (12,000 each of the 12 tribes of Israel. (Rev. 7:5-8)

The 144,000 are:

1. Jews. (from the 12 tribes of Israel)

2. Servants of God. (Rev. 7:3)

3. They are specifically selected of God for a particular purpose (Rev. 14:1-4). Their message will be: "Endure, to the end", and then Christ will return.

4. They will have a special place/status/position. (Rev. 14:3, 7:9, 13 & 14)

F. The Action of the Great Tribulation

Revelation, chapters 6 – 19 covers the events to occur during the Great Tribulation.

1. The first half (3 ½ years) will be a peaceful period, as the Antichrist makes his debut, as a very knowledgeable person in world economics,

politics, military affairs, and religion. (2 Thess. 2:3, 4, & 9)

2. He will make a peace treaty with Israel, and, after 3 ½ years will break it. (Dan. 9:27, this will be in the middle of "Daniel's 70th week")

3. Then, we considered the opening of the Seals. (Rev. 6, & Rev. 8:1)

4. The 7th Seal contains the 7 Trumpets. (Rev. 8 & 9)

5. Remember, the 7th Trumpet did two things:

   a. Brings the proclamation that Christ will soon return to earth, and,

   b. Contains the 7 Vials (or, bowls)

6. Rev. 16:1-21 is the pouring of those 7 Vials.

Then we briefly looked at Daniel's interpretation of Nebuchadnezzar's dream (Daniel 2 & 7), and how it equates to the reforming of the old Roman Empire, which will result in a 10 Nation Federation; and, we looked at the False Church symbolized by the Harlot of Revelation 17 & 18)

    6. Next, is the Second Coming of Christ

Without a doubt one of the greatest events on God's prophetic calendar.

    A. Following the 7-year period of the Great Tribulation, Luke 21:25-26 tells us "the powers of heaven will be shaken".

That will be accomplished through the pouring out of the 6th and 7th Vials; and, then, a voice from heaven will proclaim, "It is Done". (Rev. 16:12-14 & 16-21)

At this point there will literally be a reshaping of the continents: Thunder, lightning, a mighty earthquake, mountain's crumbling, islands disappearing, and 100-pound hail stones falling from heaven.

    B. Then, Christ will appear, riding on a white horse; His eyes as a flame of fire, with many crowns upon His head, and His robe covered with blood. (Rev. 19:11-13)

The stables of heaven will release her horses, and all the Saints in heaven will gallop across the galaxies again, and return to earth with Christ.

    C. And Christ will descend upon the Mount of Olives (Zech. 14:3-4), and the mountain will split in two. (I believe this will happen to separate Gethsemane from the Mount of Olives.)

    D. One of His first objectives will be to go to Edom (Petra), to deliver the Jews, which have fled to there during the persecution of the Great Tribulation.

Someone will ask the question found in Zechariah 13:6, "What are these wounds in your hands?" and, then, they will realize what they have done.

    E. Then, (simultaneously) according to Zechariah 14:1-3, the largest army every assembled will gather together in a place called Har Megiddo, to go to Edom to kill the Jews.

Remember, the Antichrist, at this point, has convinced the entire world to hate the Jews.

The winning side in this battle will have no casualties.

The losing side will suffer complete and total defeat. Not because of tanks, guns, atomic or nuclear weapons, but "by the sword that comes out of the mouth of Jesus Christ". (Rev. 1:16 and 19:15 & 21)

I believe that sword is His Word. (Ephesians 6:17)

    F. The Dividing (Judgment) of the Nations (Matt. 25:31-46

It is important to remember as you re-read this: This is NOT the Great White Throne Judgment.

    G. Then, finally, at His Second Coming, His dealing with the Fallen Angels. (1 Co. 6:3)

Now, remember, this period of the Second Coming, that we are looking at here, precedes the Millennial Reign.

It appears as though there will be a period of 45 days here, that Christ will "get things ready" for the Millennial Reign. (We did the math in Daniel 12:11-12)

7. Millennial Reign (Please note: This is not heaven)

A. What will it be like for Satan?

He will be shut up, sealed, chained in the Bottomless Pit (Rev. 20:1-3); and, although he will not be able to influence people, they will still have a sin nature.

B. What will it be like for our Savior?

1) He will ensure this is a time of peace. (Isa.2:4, Ho. 2:4, Micah 4:3, Zech. 9:10)

2) He will restore agricultural Conditions. (Isa. 2:4 & Micah 4:3)

3) He will provide Comfort. (Isa. 12:1 & 51:3, A Garden of Eden Environment.)

4) He will administer perfect Justice. (Isa. 9:7)

5) He will end Sickness and Disease. (Isa. 29:17-19)

6) He will make sure proper instruction is given to all people. (Jer. 3:14-15 and Micah 4:2)

C. What will the Millennial Reign be like for the Saints?

1) We will (physically) be with the Lord. (1 Thess. 4:17)

2) We will reign with Christ, to administer the affairs of the world of those things in "B" above. (2 Tim. 2:11-12, Rev. 20:4-6, Rev. 3:21, Rev. 2:26-27)

3) We are going to worship Jesus Christ. (Isa. 66:23 and Zech. 14:16)

D. What will it be like for the Survivors?

1) They will continue to live in their natural physical bodies.

2) They will continue to reproduce. (Eze. 47:22)

3) They will suffer punishment for disobedience. (Isa. 66:24)

4) They will labor. (Isa. 65:21-23)

5) They will be prosperous. (Eze. 36:29-38)

6) They will speak one language. (Zeph.3:9)

E. What will it be like for the Earth?

1) It will be restored, and the original curse lifted. (Amos 9:13)

2) Animal life will be changed. (Isa. 11:6-9)

3) And, I believe there will be a single land mass, caused by the Great Tribulation and the Second Coming.

F. What will it be like for Israel?

1) They will have a restored relationship with God. (Isa. 62:2-5)

2) They will be exalted above the Gentiles. (Isa. 62:2-5)

3) They will become God's witnesses, as children are being born, and will need to be taught. (Zeph. 3:20)

G. What will it be like for the Sanctuary?

1) There will be a temple. (Isa. 2:3, also Eze. 40-48 describes the new temple in detail)

2) Sacrifices will again be made, to teach the children born, about "Atonement". (Isa. 56:5-7 and 60:7)

8. Next, we studied Satan's Last Stand

A. Remember during the Millennial Reign he has been in the Bottomless Pit. (Rev. 20:1-3)

B. He will be "loosed a little season", to try to persuade the "Kingdom Kids" to join him to overthrow Christ. God always gives us a choice. (verse 3)

C. And, Satan will be successful in deceiving many. (Rev. 20:8) "As the sand of the sea". Can you imagine enduring the Great Tribulation, and then being deceived here?

D. The Results of his deception? (Rev. 20:9)

　1) Death to his followers.

　2) Total and Complete Victory for the Saints.

E. The 2nd Result?

　Satan will be cast into the Lake of Fire. (Rev. 20:10)

9. Which brings us to: The Great White Throne Judgment

A. The Judge of the Throne: Jesus Christ. (John 5:22 & 27, Acts 10:40-42, 2 Tim. 4:1)

B. The Journey to the Throne, for all people, from all time, and all places. (Rev. 20:13)

C. The Jury of the Throne. (Rev. 20:12, and other books)

　1) The Book of Conscience (Rom. 2:14-15)

　2) The Book of Words (Matt. 12:36-37)

　3) The Book of Secret words and works (Rom. 2:16 & Eccl. 12:14)

　4) The Book of Public Works (2 Co. 11:15 & Matt. 16:27)

　5) The Book of Life (Phil. 4:3, Rev. 20:12 &15, 21:27)

D. The Judged of the Throne.

1) The lost (unsaved) (Rev. 20:15)

2) and, I believe the saved, Kingdom Kids. (Where else would they be judged?)

E. The Judgment of the Throne.

The Second Death, a life sentence in the Lake of Fire (Rev. 20:14-15)

10. The Eternal State

A. Heaven and Earth will pass away (Rev. 21:1-2 & 2 Peter 3:10-13), and there will be a new Heaven, new Earth, and new Holy City Jerusalem.

B. The earth will experience a cleansing by fire, and will become "new"

1) There will be no more sea. (Rev. 21:1 & 22:1)

2) There will be no more hell. (Matt. 25:30)

3) There will be no more sin. (Isa. 65:17)

4) There will be no more tears. (Rev. 21:25 & Zech. 14:7)

C. And we considered the New Jerusalem.

1) Its tremendous size (Rev. 21:16)

2) Its unique "rainbow colored" foundation (verses 19 & 20)

3) Its walls of Jasper (verses 17 & 18)

4) Its Pearly Gates (verses 12, 13, & 21)

5) Its Golden Street (singular) (verse 21)

6) Its bright Light, Who is Christ. (verse 23)

7) It will have a Pure River and Tree of Life (Rev. 22:1-2)

But it will not have a temple (Rev. 21:22), because people will gather to worship at the feet of Jesus Christ.

**"The grace of our Lord Jesus Christ
be with you all. Amen."
Rev. 22:21**

Ray James

Nearing The End of the Beginning

Ray James

www.ingramcontent.com/pod-product-compliance
Lightning Source LLC
Chambersburg PA
CBHW052057110526
44591CB00013B/2251